STUDY GUIDE

TO ACCOMPANY

HUMAN SEXUALITY
Diversity in Contemporary America
Third Edition

by Bryan Strong, Christine DeVault, and Barbara Werner Sayad

Developed by

Bobbi Mitzenmacher, MS
California State University, Long Beach

Barbara Werner Sayad, MPH, CHES
California State University, Monterey Bay

Mayfield Publishing Company
Mountain View, California
London • Toronto

International Standard Book Number: 0-7674-0514-5

Manufactured in the United States of America

10 9 8 7 6 5 4 3 2 1

Mayfield Publishing Company
1280 Villa Street
Mountain View, California 94041
(650) 960-3222

Cover Photo: © Diane Fenster

Text Credits
Page 68   Reprinted by permission from *The Marriage and Family Experience,* 7th edition by Brian Strong, Christine DeVault, and Barbara Sayad. Copyright © 1998 by Wadsworth Publishing Company.
Page 78   Adapted from Maxine Baca Zinn and D. Stanley Eitzin, *Diversity in Families,* 2nd edition, Harper and Row, 1990. With permission from Addison-Wesley Educational Publishers.

 This book is printed on recycled paper.

A MESSAGE TO STUDENTS

This Study Guide is designed to help you achieve two important goals in learning about human sexuality. First, it will make it easier for you to study, review, and comprehend the material you are learning from the textbook, *Human Sexuality,* Third Edition, by Bryan Strong, Christine DeVault, and Barbara Sayad. Although it is true that each of us already possesses some knowledge about human sexuality, you may be surprised by the amount of new information as well as the number of terms and ideas that will be presented in your class and the textbook. This Study Guide aims to increase your success in learning, retaining, and integrating the essential information.

Second, but of equal importance, this Study Guide will give you opportunities to think about human sexuality, research, and issues in the context of your own life. Sexuality is not just about sexual activity. It is a matter that affects your biological, psychological, cultural, and ethical makeup. More than any other class you will take in college, the ideas you will be learning about, the objective information that is presented, and the applications that are possible have the potential to affect your future behavior and personal development.

To help you focus on important concepts, each chapter of the Study Guide begins with a set of Learning Objectives, which you may wish to review. The Study Guide also lists key terms as they appear in the text. Definitions for these are in the textbook as well as the Glossary, located at the end of the book. Each chapter also includes a practice test of multiple choice, true/false, fill-in, and short answer questions that test your knowledge of key terms and concepts presented in the textbook. Note that Part IV of this book contains the answers, or page references to the answers, to the test questions. You may wish to give special attention and additional review to any questions that you missed or feel uncertain about, even if you did guess the correct answer. Approximately 30% of the practice test questions also appear in the instructor's test bank.

The remaining sections are designed to help make the class content more relevant and meaningful. "Observation" exercises provide out-of-class opportunities to relate information about sexuality to your background knowledge or observations. Exercises may include conducting an interview, observing and recording people's behavior in a public setting, or watching a TV program or commercial to gain insight into the messages that are being sent about males and females, relationships, and sexual behavior. To help apply material to your own experience, the "Reflection" sections include exercises, assessments, and questions for analyzing how information in the chapter relates to your experience, behavior, and opinions.

"Gender and Sexual Identity Questions" are located at the end of each chapter. Each group contains questions to answer and open-ended statements for you to complete. Based on our observations and feedback by thousands of students, this very personal and revealing exploration is likely to provide you with meaningful insights and personal awareness and growth. You may wish to keep your comments and answers to these exercises in a private place. Following the "tour" of your textbook, there is a further explanation about how you can use these exercises to help write an essay that will lead you to reflect and learn more about your own sexual and gender identity.

Part III of the guide consists of a summary of resources for reading and writing about human sexuality. It is intended to support any handouts your instructor may provide and offer a framework from which you can prepare your research. Supplement this with concepts presented in Chapter 2 of the Mayfield Quick View Guide to the Internet for Students of Intimate Relationships, Sexuality, and Marriage and the Family, and your own critical thinking, and you can begin to explore the complex and fascinating subject of human sexuality.

Each student comes to this class with a unique background and feelings about sexuality and its place in his or her life. We hope that your efforts in completing the following activities will provide new insights and, more importantly, encourage you to re-examine your attitudes and behaviors with regard to sexuality and its place in your life.

CONTENTS

PART I

INTRODUCTION

GETTING TO KNOW YOUR TEXTBOOK:
A SELF-GUIDED TOUR

Over the next few months, you'll be spending considerable time with your textbook. Along with lectures and discussions, the textbook will be one of your most important learning tools. The authors have given much thought to how the various elements of the textbook fit together. These different elements form a whole, whose aim is to further your understanding of human sexuality.

The authors have designed the questions below to provide you with a self-guided learning tour through the textbook. (Most examples will be taken from Chapter 1.) You will explore each element. When you have completed this tour, you will be able to use the textbook to its full advantage.

As you answer each question, write down your responses on a separate sheet of paper. Your responses should be very brief, usually not more than a sentence or two. Your instructor may want you to turn them in.

First, take a few minutes to browse through the textbook to get a feel for it. What is your first impression of the book?

Read the Prologue. The section entitled "The Author's Perspective" describes several themes in the textbook. Briefly list the themes.

Read through the table of contents. This gives you an overview of what the textbook will cover. What is the title of the chapter that looks most interesting to you?

Each chapter begins with an outline that succinctly describes its structure. Read the outline to get an idea of what the chapter will cover.

You'll find a chapter summary after the main body of text in each chapter. BEFORE you read the chapter text, read the summary for Chapter 1. Reading the summary will make reading the chapter easier.

On nearly every page you'll find key terms and their definitions. These important terms are in bold-face type in the text and are summarized in the paragraph when they first appear. Find the first key term and its definition in Chapter 1. Some students find it helpful to prepare flashcards of the key terms while studying for examinations. You may wish to check with your instructor to see how useful this practice might be. Key terms are also listed alphabetically and defined in the Glossary at the end of the book.

At the end of each chapter you'll find a "Suggested Reading" section. What is the title of the book that looks most interesting to you? You can look here if you want to do more research on a subject now for your class or in the future when you would like to know more about a particular subject.

Each chapter has one or more boxes entitled either "Practically Speaking," or "Think About It." These go into a subject in greater depth or provide you with another way of looking at things. Read the first box, "My Genes Made Me Do It: Sociobiology, Evolutionary Psychology, and the Mysteries of Love." Were you able to penetrate the illusions which were portrayed?

The authors have carefully selected the photographs, charts, and tables to reinforce chapter material. On which page do you find the most interesting photograph in this chapter? Why do you find it interesting?

Because this textbook is based on scholarly research, you'll find that after the authors present important ideas or research findings they cite (identify) the source of the statements. These citations follow the style recommended by the American Psychological Association. The citations are placed in parenthesis, with the author's name and date of publication, i.e., (Strong, DeVault, and Sayad, 1999). You will find the full bibliographic citation for these sources at the back of the textbook in the Bibliography. Find the first citation in Chapter 1 and look it up in the Bibliography. What is its full bibliographic citation?

There is also a detailed index to help you find your way around in this textbook. Look up a couple of topics that interest you in the index, write down their page references, and then turn to those pages in the text. What were the topics you looked up?

Finally, list the three most important things you learned about human sexuality or yourself after reading this chapter.

GENDER AND SEXUAL IDENTITY: AN EXPLANATION

Though the goals and objectives of each human sexuality course differ, one theme that unites all of them is the application of the information and concepts presented in class to students' attitudes, beliefs, values, and behavior.

We are aware that in asking you to describe the various influences on your personal sexual identity and the impact they have had on your sexual attitudes and behaviors, a variety of challenges and obstacles may arise. First is the confusion that results from the barrage of conflicting messages and their interpretations. Second are the uncomfortable and sometimes painful feelings that may result from articulating and confronting certain experiences, perhaps for the first time. Third is the discomfort that occurs from revealing such personal issues to a stranger, that is, the instructor, for the purpose of receiving a grade. And fourth is the issue of how to proceed with your life once this information has been revealed. We hope that doing this exercise will give you a chance to clarify your feelings and reduce the confusion and discomfort that may be associated with self-exploration. The support and encouragement of your instructor and close friends as well as the services of the university's counseling center may also be helpful if you find that responding to the statements unleashes feelings that are difficult for you to deal with. Above all, you have the right to choose whether or not to participate. If you choose not to, consider putting the questions aside until a later date when you are ready.

In spite of these profound issues, we have found, over the years of teaching human sexuality courses, that this assignment is the most valuable experience of our students' semester. Students who choose to participate report insights that, they say, would not otherwise have occurred. Though many have discovered that it is no easy task to break the patterns and deeply ingrained beliefs that they have held since childhood, this exercise encourages them to consciously work toward improving them.

One former student wrote:

> The assignment really pushed me to take a closer look at my inner self—at what my opinions and values really are, and how people and the society around me influenced my development without my being conscious of it. Things came up that I had forgotten about, and it made me realize that I had to face my problems. I never knew that such feelings of resentment, insecurity, and happiness were there. I know the things I learned here will be beneficial to me throughout my life.

Begin by answering the questions on pages 7 and 8. Not all of these questions are appropriate for everyone's situation, so you can be selective in your responses. Next, after you've read the chapter in your textbook and finished the other exercises, complete the "Gender and Sexual Identity Questions" that appear at the end of each chapter. Conclude this assignment by summarizing key elements of your gender and sexual identity according to the essay description on page 6.

If you choose to take the opportunity that this self-exploration activity provides, we believe that a meaningful dimension of this course will be fulfilled.

Notice that personal statements written by students follow each chapter's gender and sexual identity assignment. Students allowed us to use these quotes in the study guide because they agreed that sharing them may help increase other people's awareness and sensitivity to sexual identity issues. We hope you find them helpful.

GENDER AND SEXUAL IDENTITY ESSAY

As you go through the study guide, you will have the opportunity to answer the gender and sexual identity questions at the end of each chapter. This will give you a chance to consider your behaviors and beliefs and the positive and negative experiences that have influenced your personal sexual identity.

After working with these pages, you may want to write an essay to help you put all of this material about yourself together. You can organize it by looking at some of these issues that may have been important to you:

- religious upbringing

- school/educational experiences and/or teachers

- peers or friends

- the media (music, TV, magazines, movies, etc.)

- parents and family

- cultural or ethnic background (including travel)

- other aspects, such as past relationships

Depending on how much exposure you have had to psychology, you may find it helpful to relate the following core issues in people's lives to the above areas:

- control/power and boundaries

- trust

- self-esteem

- fear of rejection/abandonment

- grieving for ungrieved losses

- resolving conflicts

- giving and receiving love or being intimate

Your essay should be five to seven pages in length and address the impact each of these factors has had on you in your experiences and observations. Your essay should include your age and culture, the number and sex of children in your family, where you are in the birth order (oldest, youngest, etc.), and your parents' marital status.

The conclusion should summarize key positive and negative experiences and possible constructive ways one can, should, or does cope with negative experiences to help shape a more positive sexual identity.

Title your essay. Try to find an interesting and creative title that reflects your key issue, challenges, or successes. Past titles from our students have been "Caught Between Two Cultures," "Being Taught to Hate . . . Yourself," "The Long and Winding Road," "Family, Friends, Faith, and Fairy Tales," "Turning Point," "The Freak Boy Within," and "Three Dads, Two Moms, and a Kid." Use your imagination!

BACKGROUND INFORMATION FOR
GENDER AND SEXUAL IDENTITY ESSAY

These are some of the facts and reflections that should be incorporated into your gender identity paper.

1. My age is _____.

2. My gender is: Male _____ Female _____

3. My birth order is _____ (oldest, youngest, middle, only child).

4. The number of siblings in my family are:

    Brothers _____ Sisters _____ Stepbrothers _____ Stepsisters _____

5. My parents are: Married _____ Divorced _____ Separated _____

    Deceased (one or both parents) _____ Never married _____

6. My feelings about my parents' marital status are _____.

7. My marital status is: Single _____ Cohabitating _____ Engaged _____ Married _____

    Divorced or separated _____ Widowed _____

8. My feelings about my marital status are _____.

9. I am _____ am not _____ sexually active.

10. My feelings about this include _____.

11. My sexual orientation is _____.

12. My living arrangements involve _____.

13. The relationship I value most is with _____

    because _____.

14. The relationship I value least is with _____

    because _____.

15. My ethnic background on my mother's side is _____.

16. This has affected me by _____.

17. My ethnic background on my father's side is _____.

18. This has affected me by _____.

19. Concerning my ethnic background, I feel _____ .

20. I would describe my parents' marital relationship as being _____ .

21. My parents' sexual relationship is probably _____ .

22. The impact my parents' marital and sexual relationship has had on me includes _____ .

23. Concerning my sexuality, the expectations that my parents have had for me include _____ .

24. I have fulfilled some of these expectations by _____ .

25. I have not fulfilled some of these because _____ .

26. Concerning my parents' expectations of me, I feel _____ .

27. In relation to my parents' sexual values, I feel _____ .

28. I have handled these differences by _____ .

29. I would describe my relationship with my mother as being _____ .

30. I would describe my relationship with my father as being _____ .

31. I would describe my relationship with another significant authority figure as being _____ .

32. My religious training was _____ .

33. My current religion is _____ .

34. I handle any difference between my parents' religious teachings and my own practices and beliefs

    by _____ .

35. Religion has brought to my life _____ .

36. The most significant factor that has influenced my sexual being is _____ .

(Keep these questions and refer back to them throughout your self-exploration.)

PRETEST: WHAT'S YOUR SEX IQ?

Do this pretest before you start reading the textbook to see what your basic knowledge is about some of the many fascinating things you'll be learning about this semester.

(IT'S FUN TO TEST YOUR FRIENDS ON THIS!—AND SPREAD A LITTLE KNOWLEDGE)

Mark T or F on the line before the question.

_____ 1. A female can become pregnant during sexual intercourse without the male having an orgasm.

_____ 2. After exposure to HIV, most individuals will test positive within one month.

_____ 3. If a female is a virgin, she will have a hymen intact.

_____ 4. A majority of the sexual crimes against children are committed by adults who are friends or relatives of the victim.

_____ 5. The volume of semen consists primarily of sperm.

_____ 6. A female must experience orgasm in order to become pregnant.

_____ 7. A female can become pregnant the first time she has sexual intercourse.

_____ 8. Alcohol is a common cause of temporary impotence.

_____ 9. An imbalance of sex hormones is the most frequent cause of homosexuality.

_____ 10. Among married couples in the United States, birth control pills are the most popular method of birth control.

_____ 11. Male transvestites (men who like to dress in women's clothes) are usually homosexual.

_____ 12. A large majority of parents want their children to be given sex education in the schools.

_____ 13. A person must have symptoms of AIDS to infect others.

_____ 14. The age at which puberty starts has stayed constant over the last 200 years.

_____ 15. It is possible for a woman to become pregnant during her period.

_____ 16. The most common sexually transmitted disease among college students is gonorrhea.

_____ 17. A man usually expels more than 200 million sperm in each ejaculation.

_____ 18. Fertilization of the egg (conception) occurs in the vagina.

_____ 19. About 80% of the women with chlamydia have no visible symptoms of the disease.

_____ 20. Testicular cancer primarily affects men over 50.

_____ 21. In all countries, AIDS is mainly a disease of male homosexuals.

_____ 22. For most women, birth control pills have more benefits than negative health effects.

_____ 23. Alcohol and marijuana are sexual stimulants.

_____ 24. Teenage girls have easier pregnancies and healthier babies.

_____ 25. Herpes simplex type II can be cured.

_____ 26. Home screening tests are now available for HIV.

_____ 27. Women can get pregnant without penetration of the vagina.

_____ 28. The HIV virus can be transmitted by oral sex.

_____ 29. Nocturnal emissions ("wet dreams") are often an indication of a sexual problem.

_____ 30. The amount of vaginal lubrication is a reliable indicator of a woman's sexual interest.

_____ 31. The practice of female circumcision was halted long ago.

_____ 32. Most transsexuals feel that they really should be a member of the other sex.

_____ 33. Children first become sexual when they reach puberty.

_____ 34. Masturbation can be harmful if it occurs more than twice a week.

_____ 35. Statutory rape means forced intercourse between an adult and a child or teenager.

_____ 36. Most people who have had sexual experience during childhood or adolescence with someone of the same sex will become gay or lesbian.

_____ 37. People who live together before marriage tend to divorce less often than those who did not live together before their marriage.

_____ 38. Infants are capable of erection or vaginal lubrication.

_____ 39. The greatest increase in the number of people testing positive for HIV since 1990 is among gay white men.

_____ 40. Oral-genital contact between a husband and wife is illegal in some states.

Pretest answers and short explanations appear on the following pages.

ANSWERS TO PRETEST: WHAT'S YOUR SEX IQ?

1. True—The little bit of fluid that comes from the Cowper's gland before a man ejaculates can contain sperm and cause pregnancy. It doesn't happen often, but who wants to take a chance?

2. False—The vast majority of individuals who are exposed to HIV will test positive within six months.

3. False—The hymen can be torn as girls grow up, and sometimes females are born without a complete hymen.

4. True—Most often it is friends and relatives, not strangers, who molest children.

5. False—Most of semen is fluids from the seminal vesicles and prostate gland, so despite the fact that there are millions of sperm, it only makes up a small percentage of the total ejaculate.

6. False—A woman does not have to have an orgasm to get pregnant.

7. True—Sperm and eggs don't care if it is the first time. If they meet, conception can take place.

8. True—alcohol can cause temporary impotence. While it lowers inhibitions and makes us less likely to think of all the consequences, alcohol can cause physical sexual problems. The social expectations we have learned looking at sexy liquor commercials and billboards probably have a lot to do with the images and expectations we have for ourselves.

9. False—We really don't know why people are gay or lesbian, but their hormone level does not seem to be a factor. There is some evidence that points to genetics as playing a part.

10. False—Among married couples sterilization, including vasectomy for males and tubal ligation for females, is the most popular method of birth control.

11. False—Transvestites are not usually homosexual.

12. True—Surveys show most parents want schools to provide sex education; however, the people who oppose sex education receive a great deal of publicity in the media. There is also controversy about what should be covered.

13. False—You do not have to have symptoms of AIDS to infect others.

14. False—Over time, puberty has occurred at a younger age. Two hundred years ago menstruation stated about age 17; the average age now is 12 or 13. We think part of the difference can be attributed to better nutrition.

15. True—While the risk is low, an egg can be put into a woman's system at any time, and if it meets with a sperm, she can become pregnant.

16. False—The most common sexually transmitted diseases among college students are chlamydia and genital warts.

17. True—Isn't that amazing!

18. False—Fertilization usually takes place in the fallopian tubes.

19. True—Women, more often than men, have no visible symptoms of chlamydia, until serious complications have arisen.

20. False—Though testicular cancer is rare, it primarily affects men from ages 20–35. Prostate cancer is the more common type of cancer we see in older men.

21. False—In many countries, the number of men and women affected are equal.

22. True—While some women should not take birth control pills because of their age or preexisting medical problems, most women have more positive than negative effects.

23. False—In reality, alcohol and marijuana are depressants—but they do lower inhibitions as discussed in the answer to question 8.

24. False—Teenagers who are pregnant have riskier pregnancies and more health problems. Unfortunately, they often don't get good prenatal care.

25. False—Although there is a drug that can decrease the severity and pain associated with an outbreak of herpes simplex type II, the herpes virus stays in the body throughout a person's lifetime.

26. True—Even though the test may be quite accurate for detecting HIV infection, inadequate counseling, a false sense of security if the test turns out negative, and insufficient information about the risk of other STDs are issues which concern health-care providers.

27. True—While rare, sperm deposited close to the vagina have caused pregnancies.

28. True—Though uncommon, the virus that causes AIDS can be transmitted by oral sex when infected semen or vaginal secretions get into open sores or cuts in and around the mouth.

29. False—Nocturnal emissions are a normal occurrence in men.

30. False—While vaginal lubrication can be an indicator of a woman's arousal, it is only a *first sign,* and further communication is important. Other factors, like taking medicines and menopause, can lower lubrication.

31. False—Unfortunately, female circumcision is still practiced in parts of the world.

32. True—Transsexuals usually feel like they are "trapped" inside the wrong body.

33. False—It is normal for children to masturbate and have sexual feelings at a very young age.

34. False—Other than guilt that may be associated with it, masturbation does not have harmful physical or psychological effects.

35. False—Even if a minor is willing, statutory rape can be charged when an adult has intercourse with a minor. (In many states this law applies only when *minor-aged women* have sex with *adult men.*)

36. False—Studies show that many people have same-sex experiences while growing up and are heterosexual as adults.

37. False—Contrary to what was expected, people who cohabitate first are not less likely to divorce. It may not mean that these couples are unhappier than those that stay married, but rather that they tend to be less conservative than couples that don't cohabitate before marriage.

38. True—These are both responses that happen normally and naturally to infants.

39. False—At the present time minorities are getting AIDS at an increasing and disproportionate rate, and we are seeing more cases in women and infants.

40. True—Though not enforced, sodomy laws in some states ban oral-genital contact in all situations, including between married couples.

PART II

CHAPTER MATERIALS

CHAPTER 1
PERSPECTIVES ON HUMAN SEXUALITY

LEARNING OBJECTIVES

At the conclusion of Chapter 1, students should be able to:

1. Discuss the dissemination of sexual images through the mass media, including men's and women's magazines and advertising.

2. List the different television genres and describe how each genre portrays sexuality.

3. Describe depictions of sexuality in Hollywood films, including gay/lesbian relationships.

4. Discuss the nature of anonymous sexual interaction facilitated by the Internet and phone pornography.

5. Describe and compare the sexual impulse as seen among the Mangaia, Dani, and Victorian Americans.

6. Discuss same-sex relationships in ancient Greece and among contemporary Sambians as examples of cultural variation.

7. Describe cultural variability of gender concepts, especially in terms of transsexuality and two-spirits.

8. Discuss the concepts of nature and natural sexual behavior in relationship to societal norms.

9. Describe the emergence of the concept of normal sexual behavior, including the four criteria used to define it.

10. Explain the concepts of sexual behavior and variation in terms of continuum and nonconformity.

11. Recognize and define the key terms listed below.

Key Terms

norms	homosexuality	normal sexual behavior
sexual impulses	gender	sexual variation
sexual orientation	transsexuals	deviant sexual behavior
heterosexuality	two-spirit	fellatio
		cunnilingus

PRACTICE TEST QUESTIONS

(For answers see Part IV of this book.)

Multiple Choice

1. Advertising uses the sexual sell to promise:
   a. romance and sex.
   b. popularity.
   c. fulfillment.
   d. all of the above

2. Other than peers, the most important source of sexual knowledge for American adolescents and college students is the:
   a. educational system.
   b. family.
   c. media.
   d. church.

3. Situation comedies deal with what aspect of sexual behavior?
    a. power and dominance
    b. deviant or uncommon forms of sexual expression
    c. violation of mild taboos
    d. non-stereotypic gender roles

4. Which television genre has the most overt references and presentations of sexual behavior?
    a. sitcoms
    b. soap operas
    c. crime/action-adventures
    d. cartoons

5. Gay men and lesbian women in film:
    a. are generally absent from mainstream films.
    b. are consistently defined in terms of their sexual orientation.
    c. are generally stereotyped.
    d. all of the above are true

6. It has been suggested that reading romance novels may be a substitute for:
    a. reliable sex information.
    b. actual sex.
    c. pornography.
    d. going to the movies.

7. When we label a particular sexual behavior as unnatural or abnormal, we are:
    a. violating the laws of science.
    b. demonstrating a high level of moral development.
    c. making a value judgment.
    d. behaving like psychologists.

8. Culture:
    a. is a powerful force that molds and shapes our sexual impulses.
    b. in America appears to be irrelevant in shaping or molding our sexual behavior.
    c. has its most profound impact on our sexuality when we are children.
    d. is not subject to change over time.

9. Marriage between members of the same sex is:
    a. recognized in 15 to 20 cultures throughout the world.
    b. universally condemned.
    c. only condoned between men.
    d. universally accepted by nearly all cultures.

10. Which of the following ways of classifying sexual behavior is not considered to be a value judgment?
    a. natural-unnatural
    b. normal-abnormal
    c. moral-immoral
    d. typical-atypical

11. Most sex researchers believe that a helpful way to view particular sexual behaviors is in terms of their:
    a. typicality or atypicality.
    b. deviancy or conventionality.
    c. normality or abnormality.
    d. reproductive potential.

12. The role of sex researchers is to:
    a. describe sexual behavior.
    b. evaluate sexual behavior as good or bad, moral or immoral.
    c. help the individual form ethical and moral judgments about sexuality.
    d. establish cultural boundaries for acceptable behavior.

True/False

Mark T or F on the line before the question.

_____ 1. The media's portrayal of such issues as condom use, loving gay and lesbian relationships, and masturbation has kept pace with the wide range of other sexually explicit behaviors that are portrayed.

_____ 2. Media images of sexuality permeate all areas of life.

_____ 3. Mass media depictions of sexuality are meant to inform, not necessarily to entertain.

_____ 4. Each genre has the same formula for what is sexually permissible and how to depict sex.

_____ 5. What we have learned to call "natural" in our culture may be viewed as "unnatural" in other cultures.

_____ 6. All cultures divide human beings into only two genders: male and female.

_____ 7. All cultures assume that adults have the potential for becoming sexually aroused and for engaging in sexual intercourse for the purpose of reproduction.

_____ 8. The sex researcher Alfred Kinsey stated that normal sexual behavior is the sexual behavior a culture defines as normal.

_____ 9. In the nineteenth century, white middle-class American women were viewed as being asexual.

_____ 10. The Mangaia of Polynesia and the Dani of New Guinea are examples of cultures which have similar beliefs about sexual impulses..

Fill-In

Choose the correct term from the list at the end of this section.

1. Mass media depictions of sexuality provide _____ rather than information.

2. Cultural rules or standards are otherwise called _____.

3. In some cultures, a person of one sex who identifies with the other sex is called a _____.

4. Our incitements or inclinations to act sexually are called _____.

5. In contemporary American culture, the only sexual orientation that receives full-scale legitimacy

   is _____.

6. The attraction to sexual partners on the basis of sex—male or female—is commonly known as

   _____.

7. Within the United States there are approximately 15,000 individuals whose genitals and identities as

   men and women are discordant with each other. These individuals are called _____.

8. Behavior that conforms to a group's average or median patterns of behavior that has nothing to do

   with moral or psychological deviance is called _____ sexual behavior.

9. Instead of classifying behavior into what are essentially moralistic normal/abnormal and natural/unnatural categories, researchers view human sexuality as characterized by _____, or diversity.

10. To understand our sexual diversity, researchers believe that the best way to examine sexual behavior is to view our activities as existing on a _____.

continuum	sexual impulses
entertainment	sexual orientation
heterosexuality	sexual variation
normal	transsexuals
norms	two-spirit

Short Answer

1. Select and discuss how two of the various mass media commonly depict sexuality. Discuss what is sexually permissible and how sex is depicted in each of the formulas.

2. All cultures assume that adults have the potential for becoming sexually aroused and for engaging in sexual intercourse. Select and discuss how members of one particular culture express their sexuality.

3. Name and briefly define three criteria that are used to decide whether sexual behavior is labeled "normal" or "abnormal."

 **OBSERVATION**

Sex, Lies, and MTV

It is no secret that many people absorb hours of MTV and other formats of music each day. What effect does this medium have on their sexuality?

Turn on MTV during key viewing hours (3 to 10 P.M. weekdays and/or 8 P.M. to midnight on weekends) to listen to and observe the messages that are sent through the television waves. Take at least 30–45 minutes of viewing time to record the following:

1. What were the titles of the songs?

2. What were the artists' names?

3. What was the message(s) in each song?

4. What images helped to convey the message?

5. What apparel was worn? How did the men's differ from the women's?

6. What kind of body language was used? How did it reinforce the messages?

7. What else did you notice?

8. Did the videos have any content related to sexuality? If so, was its view sex-positive, sex-negative, or neutral?

9. What did you learn as a result of watching music videos?

Between songs and antics on MTV, commercials may also employ tactics that reinforce sex role stereotypes and provide calculated images of men, women, sex, and relationships. Carefully observe three advertisements while recording the following information:

1. What product was the advertiser trying to sell?

2. What images were provided to encourage vulnerability and/or desire for the product?

3. How were the men and/or women dressed?

4. What poses or images were used by the characters to sell the product?

5. What kind of background music was used?

6. Did the commercials have content related to sexuality? If so, were their views sex-positive, sex-negative, or neutral?

7. As a result of this advertisement would you buy this product? Why or why not?

REFLECTION

"Firsts" in Growing Up

Throughout the course you will be asked to recall your own experiences and feelings about sex, growing up, relationships, and so on. The following statements are intended to give you the opportunity to explore your own sexuality and to begin putting the information that you receive in this course into some context.

Use the following questions as a guide but don't feel constrained by them:

- I first recall being a boy or a girl when . . .

- What my parents told me about sex was . . .

- For me, the experience of approaching adolescence was . . .

- My family's reaction to my budding sexuality was . . .

- I began noticing the same or other sex when . . .

- The first experience I ever had that I would define as sexual was . . .

- My attitudes about sex differed from my friends when it came to . . .

- I think my sexual experiences have affected me by . . .

- What I've learned about my sexuality from recalling my history is . . .

GENDER AND SEXUAL IDENTITY QUESTIONS

The Impact of Media

The influence of the media, for some, is overwhelming, dramatic, and profound. Try to recall how movies, TV, computer-age technology, and other forms of media have affected your attitudes and behaviors as you respond to the following statements:

- The types of media that influenced my sexual identity the most were . . .

- The persons I admired the most included . . .

- The images I tried to achieve included . . .

- The media portrayed love relationships to be . . .

    This affected me . . .

- The media portrayed family relationships to be . . .

    This affected me . . .

- The most positive effect the media has had on my sexuality is . . .

- The most negative effect the media has had on my sexuality is . . .

- As a result of the media, my self-image and/or self-esteem was affected . . .

- I became aware of the impact of the media on my sexuality when . . .

Television showed me that if I had nice things that beautiful women would want me too. In one sense television also taught me how to have sex with women; not that I could see exactly how it was done but it gave me enough information to explore and figure it out. Television showed enough sex that it made me want to go out and try it myself.

—27-year-old Caucasian male

We found the movie Fast Times at Ridgemont High *on a movie channel. We were all so scared that our parents would come into the room that we kept switching the stations back and forth. We were all so excited because we felt like we were doing an awful thing. Nothing much ever came of it except that I will always remember it, being the first time I had ever seen two people have sex.*

—21-year-old Asian woman remembers what happened when she was 10

"Three's Company" made me think that sex was a nasty thing. The people on the show were always sneaking around, trying to hide something, so I thought that sexual curiosity was something that you should try to hide.

—23-year-old Caucasian reflecting on how TV affected her views on sexuality as a young adolescent

If there has been one recurring theme in my life, it's that I often look to "Hollywood" to inspire my quest for the perfect date. At the age of nineteen, it's quite a revelation for me to receive dating tips from movies like Fast Times at Ridgemont High, Can't Buy Me Love, *and* Swingers. *Television shows like "Friends" and "Beverly Hills, 90210" have also given me ideas of what relationships should be like.*

—19-year-old Caucasian male

The surroundings I grew up in affected how I viewed myself. The beautiful Southern California blonde was everywhere. The images on MTV and Seventeen *were very hard to live up to, but my friends and I would all try. While we could copy hair and makeup, having the bodies of the models was harder. We were always dieting, and one of my best friends developed an eating disorder.*

—22-year-old Caucasian female

CHAPTER 2
STUDYING HUMAN SEXUALITY

LEARNING OBJECTIVES

At the conclusion of Chapter 2, students should be able to:

1. Describe the sex information/advice genre, its function as entertainment, and how to evaluate it in conjunction with statistical data.

2. List and describe critical thinking skills, including examples of value judgments and objectivity; opinions, biases, and stereotypes; confusing attitudes and behaviors; and egocentric and ethnocentric fallacies.

3. Discuss ethical and sampling issues in sex research.

4. Describe and critique clinical, survey, observational, and experimental methods of sex research.

5. Discuss and critique the contributions of the early sex researchers, including Richard von Krafft-Ebing, Sigmund Freud, and Havelock Ellis.

6. Discuss and critique the contributions of Alfred Kinsey.

7. Discuss and critique the contributions of William Masters and Virginia Johnson.

8. Discuss findings of the 1994 National Health and Social Life Survey.

9. Discuss and critique the contributions of feminist and gay/lesbian scholars, including directions for future research.

10. Describe emerging research on African Americans, including socioeconomic status, stereotyping, subculture, and increasing numbers of unmarried adults.

11. Describe emerging research on Latinos, including diversity of subgroups, stereotyping, and assimilation.

12. Discuss emerging research on Asian and Pacific Islander Americans, with an emphasis in changing cultural traditions.

13. Recognize and define the key terms listed below.

Key Terms

sex information/advice genre	random sample	libido
objectivity	representative sample	pleasure principle
value judgments	biased samples	reality principle
cultural relativity	clinical research	superego
opinion	pathological behavior	moral principle
bias	survey research	oral stage
stereotype	observational research	anal stage
schema	participant observation	phallic stage
attitude	experimental research	latency stage
behavior	variables	genital stage
fallacy	independent variables	Oedipal complex
egocentric fallacy	dependent variables	castration anxiety
ethnocentric fallacy	correlational studies	Electra complex
ethnicity	plethysmographs	penis envy
ethnic group	strain gauge	social construction
scientific method	neuroses	control group
induction	repression	socioeconomic status
informed consent	psychoanalysis	cultural equivalency perspective
sample	id	machismo
		acculturation

PRACTICE TEST QUESTIONS

(For answers see Part IV of this book.)

Multiple Choice

1. The purpose(s) of media is/are to:
   a. sell more of itself.
   b. entertain.
   c. provide how-to information and/or moralize.
   d. all of the above

2. The primary difference between the media and social scientists' research is that the media:
   a. may describe research in an over-simplified and distorted manner.
   b. often qualify their findings as tentative or limited to a certain group.
   c. must use critical information about studies in order to be accurate.
   d. will usually quote only the most credible and reliable researchers.

3. Basic to any scientific study is a fundamental commitment to:
   a. research.
   b. objectivity.
   c. ensuring that the hypothesis is correct.
   d. applying the research to human behavior.

4. A professor is conducting some research and hands out a questionnaire about sexual preferences and experiences to 100 of his students. He states that completing the questionnaire is a course requirement and counts toward the final grade. This professor may be violating the principle of:
   a. informed consent.
   b. protection from harm.
   c. debriefing.
   d. right to withdraw.

5. According to the authors, of all the ethical issues surrounding research, the most problematic one is:
   a. compatibility with funding sources.
   b. finding sufficient subjects.
   c. the use of deception.
   d. the interpretation of results.

6. Value judgments:
   a. imply how a person ought to behave.
   b. can be empirically validated.
   c. provide an objective description of the world as it exists.
   d. all of the above may be true

7. Which one of the following pairings is inaccurate?
   a. Krafft-Ebing and the case study
   b. Havelock Ellis and experimentation
   c. Alfred Kinsey and the survey
   d. Masters and Johnson and laboratory observation

8. In the survey method for collecting sexual information:
   a. people tend to be poor reporters of their own sexual behavior.
   b. the interviewers may be biased and subjective.
   c. the respondents may hesitate to reveal information.
   d. all of the above may occur

9. A major criticism of the research of Sigmund Freud includes his:
   a. puritan ethics and religion.
   b. lack of ethics.
   c. inadequate descriptions of female development and lack of empiricism.
   d. ignoring childhood sexuality.

10. The National Health and Social Life Survey of 1994 did all the following EXCEPT:
   a. showed that most Americans are fairly traditional in the bedroom.
   b. was controversial and had to be finished with non-governmental funds.
   c. was the first large-scale, carefully comprehensive survey since Kinsey.
   d. showed that most women had orgasms regularly.

11. Masters and Johnson addressed and treated sexual problems by:
   a. using behavioral therapy.
   b. suggesting shock therapy.
   c. diagnosing and treating the underlying physiological problem.
   d. classifying, describing, and treating the five stages of psychosexual development.

12. Feminist research has focused on and expanded the scope of information we have about:
   a. pornography.
   b. victimization and child abuse.
   c. sex and power.
   d. all of the above

13. According to the American Psychological Association, homosexuality:
   a. is considered a psychological disorder.
   b. is no longer considered a psychological disorder.
   c. is considered an acceptable preference only if a person does not act on it.
   d. the APA has no stand on homosexuality because the research is inconclusive.

14. Values and behavior are shaped by:
   a. culture and social class.
   b. our genetic pool.
   c. discipline and control alone.
   d. factors that we don't yet understand.

15. In understanding the differences in sexual behavior among the various Latino groups, the key factor seems to be
   a. a religious tradition.
   b. socioeconomic status.
   c. degree of acculturation.
   d. geographic concentration within the United States.

Fill-In

Choose the correct term from the list at the end of this section.

1. A media genre that transmits information and norms about sexuality to a mass audience to both inform and entertain in a simplified manner is called a _____.

2. Evaluations based on moral or ethical standards rather than objective ones are called _____.

3. The process of adaptation an ethnic group makes to the values, attitudes, and behaviors of the dominant culture is known as _____.

4. When a researcher describes a sexual behavior as it really is, and does not cloud it with his or her beliefs, prejudices, or value judgments, that researcher is demonstrating _____.

5. An _____ fallacy is the belief that one's own ethnic group, nation, or culture is innately superior to others.

6. The full disclosure to an individual of the purpose, potential risks, and benefits of participating in a research project is called _____.

7. In the scientific study of sex, samples that are not representative of the larger group are known as _____ samples.

8. A major limitation of clinical research is its emphasis on unhealthy or _____ behavior.

9. The method of research that uses questionnaires or interviews to gather information from a small group and makes inferences for a larger group is known as _____ research.

10. Sigmund Freud described five stages in psychosexual development, one of which refers to a stage in which a child exhibits interest in the genitals and is called the _____ stage.

11. Self-stimulation or erotic behavior involving only the self is called _____. This includes masturbation, erotic dreams, and sexual fantasies.

acculturation	pathological
autoeroticism	phallic
biased	sex information/advice genre
ethnocentric	survey
informed consent	value judgments
objectivity	

Matching

1. Krafft-Ebing _____

2. Sigmund Freud _____

3. Havelock Ellis _____

4. Michel Foucault _____

5. Masters & Johnson _____

6. Evelyn Hooker _____

7. Alfred Kinsey _____

a. First to use a large-scale survey/continuum to demonstrate the range of behavior that exists as it relates to sexual orientation.

b. First to explore the unconscious, leading to the development of psychoanalysis.

c. Was first to write scientifically about sexuality. Explored the origins of fetishism and sadism and found them rooted in masturbation.

d. Combined direct and laboratory observation with measurement of changes in the genitals and began treating sexual dysfunctions.

e. An early English researcher who focused on female sexuality, re-evaluated homosexuality, and helped to redefine normal sexual behavior.

f. Produced a new discourse on sexuality which united sexual knowledge and power.

g. Demonstrated that homosexuality in itself was not a psychological disorder.

Short Answer

1. List and briefly describe five guidelines that can be used to evaluate the messages that the media present to us.

2. Ethical issues are particularly important in researching the subject of sexuality. State four common issues that must be addressed and discuss why they are significant.

3. Select one ethnic group and discuss how culture affects factors in studying their sexual behavior.

 **OBSERVATION**

Research Methods

To help you understand the kinds of research available, develop a chart of methods used to conduct sexual research and identify the advantages and disadvantages of each one.

<table>
<tr><td align="center">ADVANTAGES</td><td align="center">DISADVANTAGES</td></tr>
</table>

1. Clinical research

2. Survey research

3. Observational research

4. Experimental research

What do you think would be the best type of research design for each of the following questions?

1. What is the average age of first intercourse for Americans?

2. How do most people become acquainted at bars?

3. What are the effects of alcohol on sexual response?

 **OBSERVATION**

Exploring the Internet

Learning to access information on the Internet will help you to do research for this class and others. (See Part III "Researching and Networking With Computers" for basic information; these pages also offer some tips for evaluating the sources you find.) Choose a topic that you are interested in from the material covered in our textbook. Ask for help in your school computer lab if using the Internet is new to you. Then answer the following questions:

1. How many "hits" or matches did you find for your subject? _____.
    If you receive too many, try to limit your topic to some aspect of it that interests you.

2. Look at 3 sites related to your topic and answer these questions:

    A. Were the sites worthwhile to look at? _____
        Why?

    B. What did you find on most of the sites? (i.e., information, links to other sites, personal opinions, graphics).

3. Choose one site from the 3 you looked at and answer these questions:

    A. What is the URL of the site? (This usually starts with http:)

    B. What organization or person sponsors this site?

    C. Does the site include information about when it was last updated? _____
        If yes, when was this?

    D. Describe what is at this site (i.e., information, links to other sites, personal opinions, graphics, scholarly journals).

    E. How would you rate the reliability of this resource?

    F. Would you use it as a resource if you were writing a paper on the subject?

 **OBSERVATION**

The Sexy Side of Magazines

Go to a library or through your own or a friend's magazine rack and look at the lead or cover stories of popular magazines. Find one that deals with sex. Read the article and answer the following questions:

- How was the article titled?

- Who wrote the article?

- Does the author have any credentials or background to write the article?

- What type of illustrations were used?

- If examples were used, how were they chosen, and did they represent a cross section of the population?

- Was a survey done in connection with the story? _____ If yes, does the article explain how the survey was done?

- Were other experts quoted or interviewed for the article?

- Was other research cited? How reputable did it seem?

- Did the article make any sweeping claims?

- Did the article give the information the title suggested it would?

- Given the above, do you believe what was said? Why? Why not?

- Do you think the article was written to entertain or inform?

- How did this article contribute to the marketing of the magazine?

REFLECTION

Looking at Your Values

Take a few minutes to complete the following values survey. There are no right or wrong responses. Answer as honestly as you can; usually your first thought is most accurate. After you finish, read the note at the bottom of the page. A similar list exists at the end of the book. The purpose of the class is not to change your values and opinions, but to help you to re-evaluate and fully embrace who you are and what you believe.

Today's date: _____   Male _____   Female _____

SA   CIRCLE IF YOU STRONGLY AGREE
A   CIRCLE IF YOU MODERATELY AGREE
U   CIRCLE IF YOU ARE UNDECIDED, OR HAVE NO OPINION
D   CIRCLE IF YOU MODERATELY DISAGREE
SD   CIRCLE IF YOU STRONGLY DISAGREE

STATEMENT		LEVEL OF AGREEMENT				
A.	You should have sex only with someone you love.	SA	A	U	D	SD
B.	Masturbation is a healthy, acceptable form of sexual behavior.	SA	A	U	D	SD
C.	A woman should feel able to be as sexually assertive as a man.	SA	A	U	D	SD
D.	Abortions should be available to any woman who desires to terminate a pregnancy.	SA	A	U	D	SD
E.	Transvestites are psychologically dysfunctional.	SA	A	U	D	SD
F.	Prostitution should be a crime.	SA	A	U	D	SD
G.	Magazines like *Penthouse* and *Playboy* should be available at liquor stores.	SA	A	U	D	SD
H.	Homosexuality is unnatural and immoral.	SA	A	U	D	SD
I.	High school clinics should provide birth control.	SA	A	U	D	SD
J.	All doctors should be tested for HIV, and patients notified of status.	SA	A	U	D	SD
K.	Parents should be notified and give permission before their daughters can have an abortion.	SA	A	U	D	SD
L.	All hospital patients should be tested for HIV, and doctors notified of status.	SA	A	U	D	SD
M.	If a 15-year-old boy has consensual sex with a 20-year-old female, she should be arrested.	SA	A	U	D	SD
N.	If a 15-year-old girl has consensual sex with a 20-year-old male, he should be arrested.	SA	A	U	D	SD
O.	Surrogate motherhood should be legal.	SA	A	U	D	SD
P.	Rape is often charged because women regret what they did.	SA	A	U	D	SD
Q.	A boy who has not had sex by the time he is 17 is weird.	SA	A	U	D	SD

After you complete the survey, look over your answers and ask yourself these questions.

Were your answers for J and L the same? _____

Do you think the issue for these is the same? Why do you think that?

Look at M and N. Was your answer the same? _____ Why do you think that you feel that way?

Were you undecided on many issues? _____ If yes, why do you think that is so?

GENDER AND SEXUAL IDENTITY QUESTIONS

Honesty and Sexuality

Even though gender issues don't directly relate to research, being honest about ourselves may be difficult when we're asked about sex-related issues.

If a trusted person inquired about your sexuality would you

- be perfectly honest?

- be willing to reveal all of your prior sexual experience?

- share your medical/sexual history?

- discuss your sexual fantasies?

- talk about your painful experiences?

The most difficult sexual topic for me to talk about honestly is . . .

If I was asked to share my sexual history with a researcher, I would probably . . .

This (the gender and sexual identity paper) has been a really worthwhile assignment. It made me think and reflect about who I really am. I found it really enlightening. It gave me some time to think and I needed that.
—26-year-old Hispanic female

While it was painful at points, it (the gender and sexual identity paper) helped me analyze aspects of myself that I otherwise would not have thought about, even after having taken this class. Writing about my sexual identity forced me to look more deeply into it. It has given me the strength to go into counseling to learn more about myself.
—20-year-old Asian female

CHAPTER 3
FEMALE SEXUAL ANATOMY, PHYSIOLOGY, AND RESPONSE

LEARNING OBJECTIVES

At the conclusion of Chapter 3, students should be able to:

1. List and describe the functions of the external female sexual structures.

2. List and describe the functions of the internal female sexual structures.

3. Describe the structures and processes involved in ovulation.

4. Describe the structure and function of the breasts.

5. List the principal female reproductive hormones.

6. Describe oogenesis and the phases of the ovarian cycle.

7. Describe the phases of the menstrual cycle and its interrelationship with the ovarian cycle.

8. Discuss menstruation, including cultural aspects, physical effects, and possible problems.

9. Compare and contrast Masters and Johnson's and Kaplan's models of the sexual response cycle.

10. Describe the psychological and physiological processes involved in the female sexual response, including vaginal secretions and lubrication and the role of orgasm.

11. Recognize and define the key terms listed below.

Key Terms

genitals	oocytes	ovulatory phase
vulva	ova (ovum)	luteal phase
mons pubis	ovulation	menstrual cycle
mons veneris	ovarian follicles	menstrual phase
clitoris	corpus luteum	menses
glans clitoridis	fallopian tubes	menarche
clitoral hood	urethra	proliferative phase
crura	urethral opening	secretory phase
labia majora	anus	premenstrual syndrome (PMS)
labia minora	perineum	dysmenorrhea
vestibule	pelvic floor	prostaglandins
Bartholin's glands	lactation	amenorrhea
vagina	mammary gland	Masters and Johnson's Four-Phase Model
coitus	areola	of Sexual Response
birth canal	alveoli	Kaplan's Tri-Phasic Model of
introitus	hormones	Sexual Response
hymen	gonadotropins	erogenous zones
Grafenberg spot (G spot)	estrogens	pheromones
uterus	progesterone	vasocongestion
cervix	oogenesis	myotonia
endometrium	ovarian cycle	sweating
os	gonadotropin-releasing hormone (GnRh)	tenting
ovary	follicle-stimulating hormone (FSH)	sex flush
gonad	luteinizing hormone (LH)	orgasmic platform
gametes	follicular phase	orgasm

PRACTICE TEST QUESTIONS

(For answers see Part IV of this book.)

Multiple Choice

1. An important difference between the clitoris and the penis is that the clitoris:
   a. cannot undergo erection.
   b. has no functions other than sexual pleasure.
   c. has no cover that is equivalent to the foreskin of the penis.
   d. has relatively few nerve endings compared to the penis.

2. The vulva consists of the:
   a. external female genitals.
   b. external and internal sex organs of the woman.
   c. labia minora and majora.
   d. mons pubis and clitoris.

3. Women who experience pain during their first act of intercourse tend to:
   a. be younger than those who did not.
   b. hold more conservative sexual values.
   c. have expected intercourse to be painful.
   d. all of the above are true

4. Carmen is nourishing her infant with milk produced in the
   a. alveoli.
   b. areolas.
   c. ducts.
   d. ampullae.

5. The function(s) of the ovaries is/are to:
   a. release oocytes (eggs) and produce hormones.
   b. continually manufacture oocytes and receive hormones.
   c. provide a site for pregnancy to occur.
   d. simply release eggs.

6. The most significant hormone that affects the maturation of the reproductive organs, menstruation, and pregnancy is:
   a. progesterone.
   b. estrogen.
   c. gonadotropins.
   d. testosterone.

7. Beginning with day one of the menstrual cycle, the sequence of the ovarian phase is as follows:
   a. follicular, ovulatory, and luteal.
   b. ovulatory, follicular, and luteal.
   c. luteal, ovulatory, and follicular.
   d. luteal, follicular, and ovulatory.

8. Dolores reached menarche last year. Recently she has become alarmed because she has noticed a lot of clear, slippery, stretchy secretions coming from her vagina. What may be happening here?
   a. These secretions are normal during ovulation.
   b. She may have contracted vaginismus.
   c. These are the normal signs of the sloughing off of the endometrium.
   d. These secretions indicate a normal and healthy Grafenberg spot.

9. What is the nature of the controversy that surrounds a diagnosis of premenstrual syndrome?
   a. The frequency and severity of this disorder precludes women from certain jobs.
   b. There is no clear definition or set of symptoms for this "disorder."
   c. This problem occurs only among middle-class white women.
   d. Diagnosis is complicated by dysmenorrhea.

10. Sexual intercourse during menstruation:
    a. is safe because pregnancy can never occur.
    b. is taboo in all cultures.
    c. is not pleasurable for most couples.
    d. presents certain health risks because organisms including HIV have an easier pathway into the body.

11. A criticism of the Masters and Johnson model of sexual arousal is that:
    a. it does not account for the role of desire in sexual arousal and the plateau phase cannot be distinguished from the excitement phase.
    b. it is accurate for men but not for women.
    c. each phase should be described in more detail.
    d. there is no criticism

12. Which item is out of place here?
    a. vasocongestion
    b. arousal
    c. endometriosis
    d. myotonia

13. The sex drive in both men and women is influenced by:
    a. the Bartholin's gland.
    b. testosterone.
    c. estrogen and progesterone.
    d. unknown factors.

14. The first sign of sexual excitement in women is:
    a. sweating or moistening of the vaginal walls.
    b. the tenting of the inner two-thirds of the vagina.
    c. changes in the appearance of the breasts and genitals.
    d. all of the above

15. Women:
    a. after experiencing the refractory period can once again achieve orgasm.
    b. experience multiple orgasms regularly.
    c. are physiologically able to be orgasmic immediately after orgasm.
    d. must achieve orgasm to feel emotionally satisfied and fulfilled.

Fill-In

Choose the correct term from the list at the end of this section.

1. The part of the female anatomy that contains a high concentration of nerve endings and is the center of sexual arousal is the _____.

2. Located on either side of the vaginal opening are two small ducts called the _____, which secrete a small amount of moisture during sexual arousal.

3. The opening of the vagina is known as the _____.

4. The lining of the uterine wall that is filled with tiny blood vessels and is shed during menstruation is called the _____.

5. The release of an egg from the ovary is called _____.

6. Chemical substances that serve as messengers and travel through the bloodstream to regulate various functions are called _____.

7. The pair of chromosomes that determine the genetic sex of the female is labeled _____.

8. Pelvic cramping and pain during the menstrual cycle is a condition called _____.

9. When women do not menstruate for reasons other than aging the condition is called _____.

10. Certain areas of the skin that are highly sensitive to touch and have erotic associations attached to them are called _____.

11. Chemical substances that are secreted in animals and appear to arouse sexual interest are called

    _____.

12. Another term for sex drive is _____.

13. For both males and females, the physiological changes that occur during sexual excitement depend on two processes: the swelling with blood known as _____ and muscle tension known as

    _____.

14. For women, the first sign of sexual excitement is the moistening of the vaginal walls through a process known as _____.

15. The rhythmic contractions of the vagina, uterus, and pelvic muscles accompanied by intensely pleasurable

sensations is called _____.

amenorrhea	libido
Bartholin's glands	orgasm
clitoris	ovulation
dysmenorrhea	pheromones
endometrium	sweating
erogenous zones	vasocongestion and myotonia
hormones	XX
introitus	

Short Answer

1. Briefly describe and differentiate between Masters and Johnson's and Kaplan's models of the sexual response cycle.

2. Describe the physiological changes that occur during sexual arousal in women.

3. What difference is there between the sexual response of females and males following orgasm?

FEMALE SEXUAL ANATOMY

Label the diagrams below by matching the number to the letter of the correct name.

A. INTERNAL FEMALE SEXUAL STRUCTURES

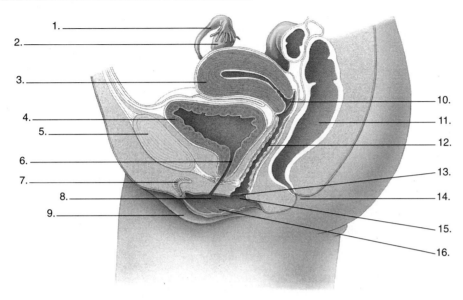

a. anus	f. labia majora	k. urethra	1. ____	6. ____	11. ____
b. bladder	g. labia minora	l. urinary opening	2. ____	7. ____	12. ____
c. cervix	h. ovary	m. uterus	3. ____	8. ____	13. ____
d. clitoris	i. pubic bone	n. vagina	4. ____	9. ____	14. ____
e. fallopian tube	j. rectum	o. vaginal opening	5. ____	10. ____	15. ____

B. EXTERNAL FEMALE SEXUAL STRUCTURES (VULVA)

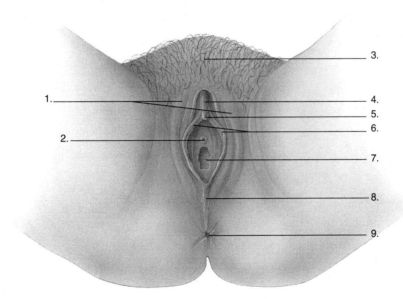

a. anus	d. labia majora	g. perineum	1. ____	4. ____	7. ____
b. clitoral hood	e. labia minora	h. opening of the urethra	2. ____	5. ____	8. ____
c. clitoris (glans)	f. mons pubis	i. vaginal opening	3. ____	6. ____	9. ____

Label the diagrams below by matching the number to the letter of the correct name. Letters may be used more than once.

C. THE FEMALE BREAST

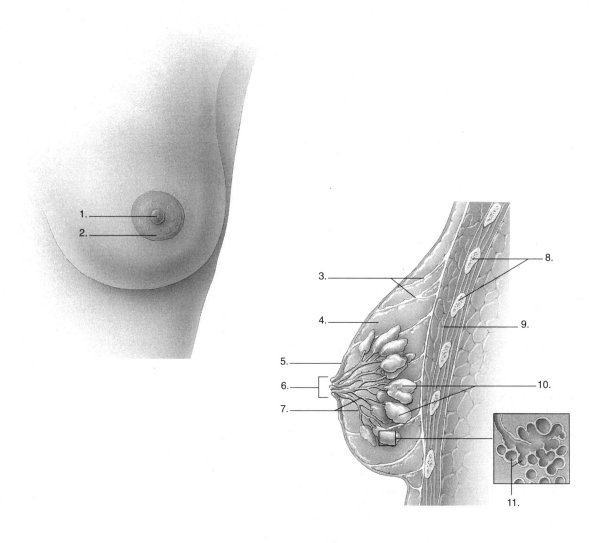

a. alveoli
b. areola
c. chest wall
d. fat
e. lobes

f. milk ducts
g. nipple
h. ribs
i. suspensory ligaments

1. _____
2. _____
3. _____
4. _____
5. _____
6. _____

7. _____
8. _____
9. _____
10. _____
11. _____

 **OBSERVATION**

Looking at Media Images

While observing advertisements (billboards, magazine ads, etc.), look for symbols representing the female genitals and breasts. What is the link between these and female sexuality? What impact do these symbols have on women's body images?

Product:

Description of advertisement:

Audience for whom it is targeted:

Message it tries to convey:

Impact on sexuality:

Discuss with three men and women their ideas and perceptions about the size of female breasts. How do their views differ and what thoughts are shared?

 **OBSERVATION**

Menstruation Attitudes

Because different cultures, genders, and generations view menstruating women from different perspectives, it might be interesting to find out how your partner, older relative, or friend from another culture views this. Keep in mind that each opinion should be valued and respected.

Before you begin asking questions, you will probably want to explain that you're taking a human sexuality course and are investigating different attitudes about menstruation.

A few sample questions that you might want to ask include the following:

- How is a menstruating woman regarded in your culture/generation?

- Are there any restrictions placed on a woman while she is menstruating?

- Is the frequency or pattern of sexual intercourse between a couple affected when the woman is menstruating?

- What are your feelings about sexual intercourse during menstruation?

- Ask a close woman friend or partner if she experiences any discomforts when menstruating. If so, what kind? When and how does she deal with them? What are her feelings about menstruation?

 **OBSERVATION**

Charting Cycles

Many women experience changes during the month that are related to their menstrual cycle. Keeping track of the symptoms they experience, especially if they suffer from PMS or dysmenorrhea, can help them, along with the help of a health professional, to find patterns and solutions. The information they record can help indicate, for instance, whether birth control pills, diet changes, exercise, and/or diet treatment would be useful. Women whose symptoms are not severe may also wish to learn more about how their menstrual cycle affects them.

The following chart provides a list of the variety of reactions women may experience. (Men may wish to share this chart with a woman if they are in a close relationship and feel this would be appropriate. Otherwise, they can save it for a time when it might be useful.) Review the chart and if you choose to keep track of symptoms (preferably for a few months), answer the questions below:

• Did you have any symptoms that you would label as severe?

• During what part of your cycle did these symptoms occur?

• Could these symptoms be attributed to other events in your life, such as stress on the job, school problems, or relationship problems? Tracking your symptoms over several months will give a better indication as to whether the symptoms are related to events in your life or if they are indeed physiological.

Day 1 Date: _____

Name: _____

Grading of menses:
- 0–none
- 1–slight
- 2–moderate
- 3–heavy
- 4–heavy and clots

GRADING OF SYMPTOMS
- 0–none
- 1–mild—present but does not interfere with activities
- 2–moderate—present and interferes with activities but not disabling
- 3–severe—disabling

DAY	1	2	3	4	5	6	7	8	9	10	11	12	13	14	15	16	17	18	19	20	21	22	23	24	25	26	27	28	29	30	31	32	33	34	35
MENSES																																			
WEIGHT																																			
Nervous tension																																			
Mood swings																																			
Irritability																																			
Anxiety																																			
Headache																																			
Craving for sweets																																			
Increased appetite																																			
Heart pounding																																			
Fatigue																																			
Dizziness or faintness																																			
Decreased coordination																																			
Depression																																			
Forgetfulness																																			
Crying																																			
Confusion																																			
Insomnia																																			
Weight gain																																			
Swelling																																			
Breast tenderness																																			
Abdominal bloating																																			
Cramps (low abdominal)																																			
Backache																																			
General aches/pains																																			

Prepared by DEL AMO HOSPITAL • 23700 Camino Del Sol • Torrance, CA 90505 • 310 530-1151

 **REFLECTION**

Female Body Image

FOR WOMEN: Looking in the Mirror

In a private location and in front of a full mirror, remove all of your clothes. Look at yourself from the front, side, and rear. Flex your muscles, slouch, and stand tall and *really* look at yourself. Do you appear firm, rounded, proportioned? What is the texture of your skin? Do you like what you see? How do you feel about your breasts? Shoulders? Backside? Legs?

Now, if you are comfortable, hold a mirror to examine your genitals closely. Can you locate each of the parts that were discussed and labeled in the book? If you like, gently touch each part of your genitals. How does it feel? What colors do you see? Did you notice something new about your genitals?

When you are ready, reflect on this experience. How comfortable were you when looking at or touching yourself? Why did you feel this way? Are you pleased with what you saw or felt? Is there anything that you might want to do to change or modify your appearance? In an intimate relationship, would you feel comfortable sharing the feelings and experiences you have about your body?

FOR MEN: Looking at Women's Bodies

Having viewed women's bodies, either in person, in a textbook, or other source, take a moment to evaluate your feelings about them.

How do you feel about the curves of a woman's body; the roundness of the breasts, hips, and buttocks? What is your reaction when you view the genitals? Can you locate each of the parts that were mentioned in the textbook? When viewing women's genitals, do you become aroused, or are you simply curious? Do you find them attractive or unattractive, or do you feel neutral about them? What do you find the most and the least attractive about a woman's body? Would you consider sharing your feelings with a partner or a trusted friend?

GENDER AND SEXUAL IDENTITY QUESTIONS

Female Body Awareness

FOR WOMEN

- The first recollection I had about my body was when . . .

- At that time, I recall feeling . . .

- When my breasts began to change, I felt . . .

- I began to menstruate when I was . . .

- When this occurred, I felt . . .

- I discussed this event with . . .

- I have/have not experienced orgasm. (I'm not sure.)

- My first orgasm occurred . . .

- When this happened, I felt . . .

- When I look at myself naked in the mirror, I feel . . .

- When my partner looks at me naked, I feel . . .

- What I like least about my body is . . .

- What I like most about my body is . . .

- I have/have not discussed my feelings about my body with my partner(s) because . . .

FOR MEN

- I began noticing that a female's body was different from mine when . . .

- At that time, I recall feeling . . .

- When I first heard about menstruation, my feelings about it were . . .

- My feelings about menstruation now are . . .

- My favorite part of a woman's body is . . .

- My least favorite part of a woman's body is . . .

- I have/have not discussed my feelings about a woman's body with my partner(s) because . . .

I attribute a great deal of my negative body image and sexual identity to the constant pressures of my childhood. I remember that they (friends) always made fun of my tummy, saying I looked pregnant (even though I was relatively small). I CANNOT look in the mirror today without seeing this huge stomach, whether it exists or not; I cannot have sex without thinking that all this man sees is my stomach. People can tell me I am beautiful daily and all I can think is that if they saw me naked they would not think so.

—27-year-old Caucasian female

I remember one day when I was about seven I was shopping with my mom. She bought Maxi pads and I asked her what they were. She said she would tell me when I was older, but she never did, and I had to learn about it from a friend.

—25-year-old female of Mexican origin

I remember as if it were yesterday when I called my mom into the bathroom telling her calmly, "I started." My dad stood in the other room saying, "Oh boy, my little girl is growing up." I felt so proud because my friends had always told me that starting your menstrual cycle was a little scary and embarrassing but for my family it was a new beginning of adulthood and I felt very comfortable with the entire episode.

—23-year-old Black female

CHAPTER 4
MALE SEXUAL ANATOMY, PHYSIOLOGY, AND RESPONSE

LEARNING OBJECTIVES

At the conclusion of Chapter 4, students should be able to:

1. List and describe the functions of the external male sexual structures.

2. List and describe the functions of the internal male sexual structures.

3. Discuss our culture's myths about the penis and compare these with myths of other cultures.

4. Discuss the male breasts and other structures that may be involved in sexual activities.

5. Discuss male sexual physiology, including sex hormones and the male cycle.

6. Discuss the role of testosterone in male behavior.

7. Explain the brain-testicular axis and compare it to the ovarian cycle.

8. Describe the process of spermatogenesis, including spermiogenesis and sex determination.

9. Describe semen production.

10. Compare and contrast male and female sexual response.

11. Describe the psychological and physiological processes involved in the male sexual response, including erection, ejaculation, and orgasm.

12. Recognize and define the key terms listed below.

Key Terms

penis	scrotum	testosterone
root	testicles (testes)	secondary sex characteristics
shaft	spermatic cord	brain-testicular axis
glans penis	seminiferous tubules	spermatogenesis
corona	epididymis	sperm
frenulum	vas deferens	spermiogenesis
foreskin	ampulla	semen
prepuce	ejaculatory duct	seminal fluid
circumcision	seminal vesicles	erection
smegma	prostate gland	ejaculation
corpora cavernosa	Cowper's glands	emission
corpus spongiosum	bulbourethral glands	ejaculatory inevitability
crura	gynecomastia	expulsion
urethra	Leygig cells	retrograde ejaculation
urethral bulb	androgens	refractory period
		erection reflex

PRACTICE TEST QUESTIONS

(For answers see Part IV of this book.)

Multiple Choice

1. In addition to a reproductive role, the male sexual organs:
   a. continually manufacture and store gametes (sperm).
   b. manufacture and release testosterone.
   c. provide a source of physical pleasure to their owner.
   d. all of the above

2. Uncircumcised men should wash the glans to:
   a. increase the production of smegma in order to increase sexual attractiveness.
   b. decrease the risk of urinary infections and penile cancer due to buildup of smegma.
   c. avoid having to be circumcised.
   d. increase production of semen.

3. Penile sizes:
   a. vary more in their flaccid state than when erect.
   b. vary more in their erect state than when flaccid.
   c. are an accurate indication of a man's virility and attractiveness.
   d. are a significant measure of sexual attractiveness for nearly all women.

4. Tom is running on a hot summer day. His scrotum is likely to:
   a. turn pale and shrink considerably.
   b. hang down with the testicles well outside the body.
   c. wrinkle and become more compact.
   d. undergo spasms due to the action of the dartos muscle.

5. The majority of the seminal fluid is produced by the:
   a. prostate.
   b. testes.
   c. seminal vesicles.
   d. vas deferens.

6. The thick clear mucus that appears on the tip of the penis before ejaculation is produced by the:
   a. Cowper's gland.
   b. prostate gland.
   c. vas deferens.
   d. epididymis.

7. Men may experience:
   a. regular fluctuation of hormone levels and mood changes.
   b. a dramatic fluctuation in testosterone production.
   c. a rapid cessation of hormones, similar to that which occurs in a female during menopause.
   d. pre-ejaculatory syndrome (PES).

8. Spermatogenesis, the production of sperm, takes place in the:
   a. prostate gland.
   b. vas deferens.
   c. seminiferous tubules.
   d. epididymis.

9. Which term most accurately describes the male and female sexual response cycle?
   a. They are very similar.
   b. They are very distinct from each other.
   c. They involve different physiological processes.
   d. Women's cycles are mosre hormonally bound.

10. Semen is relatively:
    a. acidic.
    b. alkaline.
    c. neutral.
    d. varies depending on the health of the male.

11. The penis consists of:
    a. spongy tissue.
    b. muscle.
    c. bone.
    d. all of the above

12. Nathan is diagnosed as having retrograde ejaculation. This means that
    a. his sperm count is low and he may be infertile.
    b. he is unable to attain erection during regular intercourse.
    c. he is unable to experience ejaculation and orgasm at the same time.
    d. semen passes into the bladder rather than through the urethra.

Fill-In

Choose the correct term from the list at the end of this section.

1. On the underside of the penis is a triangular area of sensitive skin called the _____.

2. The operation which surgically removes the foreskin of a male infant is called _____.

3. Beneath the foreskin of the penis are several small glands that produce an oily substance called

   _____.

4. The manufacture and release of testosterone occur in the _____.

5. The hormone that triggers sperm production and regulates the sex drive is _____.

6. The ongoing production of sperm is known as _____.

7. A feedback system called the _____ involves the pituitary gland and the testes in regulating the events of sperm production.

8. Seminal fluid, or the ejaculated liquid that contains sperm, is called _____.

9. The point at which a man feels a distinct sensation in which ejaculation must occur is termed

   _____.

10. Following orgasm, men experience a _____ during which they are not capable of becoming erect or having an orgasm again.

brain-testicular axis	semen
circumcision	smegma
ejaculatory inevitability	spermatogenesis
frenulum	testicles
refractory period	testosterone

Short Answer

1. Identify where testosterone is produced and what its various functions are, beginning with the production of secondary sex characteristics.

2. Briefly describe the route that sperm take, beginning from where they are produced to when they are ejaculated.

3. Describe the two differences that exist between men and women during the sexual response cycle.

MALE SEXUAL ANATOMY

Label the diagrams below by matching the number to the letter of the correct name.

A. INTERNAL MALE SEXUAL STRUCTURES

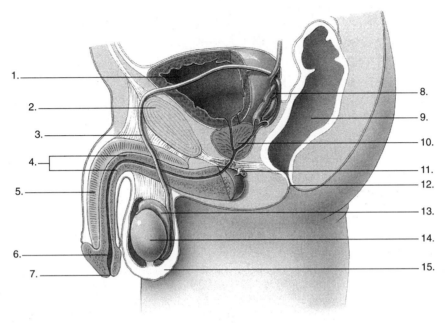

a. anus	f. opening of the urethra	k. scrotum	1. _____	6. _____	11. _____
b. bladder	g. penis	l. seminal vesicle	2. _____	7. _____	12. _____
c. corpus spongiosum	h. prostate	m. testis	3. _____	8. _____	13. _____
d. Cowper's gland	i. pubic bone	n. urethra	4. _____	9. _____	14. _____
e. epididymis	j. rectum	o. vas deferens	5. _____	10. _____	15. _____

B. EXTERNAL MALE SEXUAL STRUCTURES

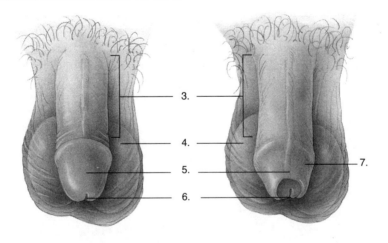

1. _____   2. _____

Label 1 and 2 either (a) circumcised or (b) intact.

c. foreskin	f. testes (in scrotum)	3. _____	6. _____
d. glans	g. opening of the urethra	4. _____	7. _____
e. shaft of penis		5. _____	

Label the diagrams below by matching the number to the letter of the correct name.

C. CROSS SECTION OF A PENIS AND A TESTICLE

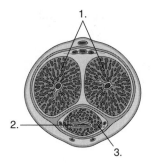

Underside of penis
(cross section)

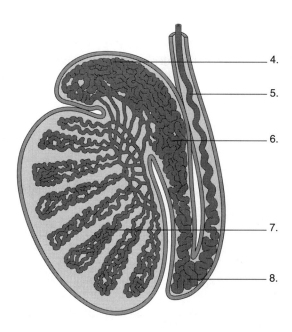

Cross section of testicle

a. corpora cavernosa
b. corpus spongiosum
c. epididymis
d. head of epididymis
e. seminiferous tubules

f. tail of epididymis
g. urethra
h. vas deferens

1. _____   5. _____
2. _____   6. _____
3. _____   7. _____
4. _____   8. _____

 **OBSERVATION**

Attitudes Toward Male Anatomy

Here are three exercises to help you reflect and clarify your views and attitudes toward male anatomy.

1. **Looking at Media Images**
    While observing advertisements (billboards, photo ads, magazines) look for symbols of the male penis. Some suggest that Joe Cool in the Camel cigarette ads is an example of this—look at his nose and chin! We have also seen an increase of male bodies, referred to as "beefcake," used to sell products in the same way that women's bodies have been used for many years. What do you think this means about changing attitudes toward male and female sexuality?

2. **Is Size Important?**
    Discuss with two men and two women their ideas and perceptions about the size of the penis. How do their views differ, and what thoughts do they share? You might also want to look in the newspaper (usually in the sports section) or in fitness magazines to see if there are ads for operations that promise to enlarge penis size.

3. **The New Baby Boy**
    A friend of yours is having a son and asks your opinion about circumcision. How would you advise your friend?

REFLECTION

You Are the Artist

On one half of a piece of paper draw a picture of a man. On the other half, a woman. (Don't worry about your artistic ability.) Try to draw the picture before reading the footnote at the bottom of the page.

Research tells us that, typically, men's heads and women's bodies are emphasized. How do your drawings compare with those findings?

 **REFLECTION**

Male Body Image

FOR MEN: Looking in the Mirror

In a private location and in front of a full mirror, remove all of your clothes. Look at yourself from the front, side, and rear. Flex your muscles, slouch, and stand tall and *really* look at yourself. Do you appear firm, rounded, proportioned? What is the texture of your skin? Do you like what you see? How do you feel about your penis? Shoulders? Backside? Legs?

Now, if you are comfortable, hold a mirror to closely examine your genitals. Can you locate each of the parts that were discussed and labeled in the book? If you like, gently touch each part of your genitals. How does it feel? What colors do you see? Did you notice something new about your genitals?

When you are ready, reflect on this experience. How comfortable were you when looking at or touching yourself? Why did you feel this way? Are you pleased with what you saw or felt? Is there anything that you might want to do to change or modify your appearance? In an intimate relationship, would you feel comfortable sharing the feelings and experiences you have about your body?

FOR WOMEN: Looking at Men's Bodies

Having viewed men's bodies, either in person, in a textbook, or another source, take a moment to evaluate your feelings about them.

How do you feel about the angles and shapes of a man's body? His shoulders, waistline, and buttocks? Do you like body hair or not? What is your reaction when you view men's genitals? Can you locate each of the parts that were mentioned in the textbook? When viewing men's genitals, do you become aroused, or are you simply curious? Do you find them attractive or unattractive, or do you feel neutral about them? What do you find the most and the least attractive about a man's body? Would you consider sharing your feelings with a partner or trusted friend?

GENDER AND SEXUAL IDENTITY QUESTIONS

Male Body Awareness

FOR MEN

- My first recollection about my body was when . . .

- At that time, I recall feeling . . .

- I experienced my first nocturnal emission when I was . . .

- When it occurred, I felt . . .

- I discussed this event with . . .

- I have/have not experienced orgasm. (I'm not sure.)

- My first orgasm occurred when . . .

- When it happened, I recall feeling . . .

- When I look at myself naked in the mirror, I feel . . .

- When my partner looks at me naked, I feel . . .

- What I like least about my body is . . .

- What I like most about my body is . . .

- I have/have not discussed my feelings about my body with my partner(s) because . . .

FOR WOMEN

- I began noticing that a male's body was different from mine when . . .

- At that time, I recall feeling . . .

- I first heard about erections when . . .

- My thoughts about it were . . .

- I first heard about nocturnal emissions when . . .

- My thoughts about it were . . .

- My favorite part of a man's body is . . .

- My least favorite part about a man's body is . . .

- I have/have not discussed my feelings about a man's body with my partner(s) because . . .

When I was around six or seven, I was still curious about other children's bodies and how they looked. One day a friend and I were in my bedroom, and I recall that we pulled our pants down to play "doctor." His mother came into the room and caught us. She acted shocked and told us to put our clothes on "right now—that's nasty!! "It's nasty" stuck in my mind for a long time.

—20-year-old Caucasian male

I had very little exposure growing up to what men or boys looked like. I remember when some friends had some Playgirl *magazines and I got my first look at male nudity. At first I was shocked and uncomfortable. However, after being in a long-term relationship I have slowly had the chance to become intimate and I now can enjoy and appreciate male anatomy!*

—23-year-old Asian female

I didn't only have sexual experiences with girls during my adolescent years. I used to also play doctor with two of my best boy-friends. I don't remember it being as enjoyable as it was with the girls though. I used to go over to Eric's house and we would orgasm off the jets in his jacuzzi. This was long before we could physically ejaculate anything.

—24-year-old Caucasian male

The summer of my eighth-grade year I had my first ejaculation while watching a pornographic movie. I have never had a wet dream. I masturbated about four times a day until I was eighteen if I wasn't having sex with a girl that day.

—25-year-old Caucasian male

CHAPTER 5
GENDER AND GENDER ROLES

LEARNING OBJECTIVES

At the conclusion of Chapter 5, students should be able to:

1. Define sex, gender, assigned gender, gender identity, gender roles, and sexual orientation and describe their differences from one another.

2. Discuss the evidence and implications for describing males and females as opposite or similar to each other.

3. Describe and critique sociobiology and gender theory and discuss the role of gender schema in creating or exaggerating female/male differences.

4. Explain cognitive social learning theory and cognitive developmental theory.

5. Describe gender-role learning from childhood through adolescence, including the major socialization influences.

6. Discuss traditional male and female gender roles and sexual scripts, including the significance of ethnicity.

7. Identify changes in contemporary gender roles and sexual scripts.

8. Define androgyny and explain how it contributes to psychological and emotional health.

9. Discuss hermaphroditism and list the major chromosomal and hormonal errors and their relationship to gender identity.

10. Discuss gender dysphoria and transsexuality, including causes and transsexual surgery.

11. Recognize and define the key terms listed below.

Key Terms

sex	cognitive social learning theory	pseudohermaphrodite
gender	cognition	Turner syndrome
assigned gender	modeling	Klinefelter syndrome
gender identity	cognitive development theory	androgen-insensitivity syndrome
gender role	peers	testicular feminization
gender-role stereotype	gender schema	congenital adrenal hyperplasia
gender-role attitude	script	DHT deficiency
gender-role behavior	androgyny	gender dysphoria
instrumentality	intersexed	transgendered
expressiveness	hermaphrodite	gender identity disorder
sociobiology		sex-typed
gender theory		sex reassignment surgery (SRS

PRACTICE TEST QUESTIONS

(For answers see Part IV of this book.)

Multiple Choice

1. For most people, biological sex, gender identity, and gender role:
   a. disagree.
   b. vary.
   c. agree.
   d. are unrelated.

2. When Sid looks at himself naked in the mirror, he feels alienated from the body he sees. He dislikes his genitals and wishes he had breasts and no penis. Sid may have confusion about his
   a. gender identity.
   b. sex.
   c. sexual orientation.
   d. genetic sex.

3. Gender, gender identity, and gender role are conceptually _____ sexual orientation.
   a. dependent on
   b. independent of
   c. co-existent with
   d. related to

4. When Terry was born, someone evaluated his _____ and said, "It's a boy!" thereby announcing his _____.
   a. genetic sex; anatomical sex
   b. gender identity; gender role
   c. anatomical sex; genetic sex
   d. anatomical sex; assigned gender

5. A woman wears perfume, dresses with ruffles, a soft hair style, and make-up. These feminine characteristics are determined by:
   a. biology.
   b. hormones.
   c. culture.
   d. chromosomes.

6. Peers provide information about gender-role norms through:
   a. play activities and toys.
   b. verbal approval or disapproval.
   c. their attitudes about various behaviors and beliefs.
   d. all of the above

7. A cognitive development theorist and a cognitive social learning theorist will agree on many things. They will DISAGREE about:
   a. the influence of culture on gender roles.
   b. adults and children learning in the same way.
   c. the role of parents in gender-role socialization.
   d. the role of modeling of behavior.

8. Processing information by gender is important in many cultures because:
   a. multiple associations between gender and non–sex-linked qualities can be made.
   b. they are a basis for norms, status, taboos, and privileges.
   c. there is no importance to processing information in this manner.
   d. a and b are both true

9. Expressions such as "men should not have certain feelings" or "performance is the thing that counts" are, according to Bernie Zilbergeld, examples of:
   a. sex-role ideals.
   b. male sexual scripts.
   c. gender-role behaviors.
   d. gender identity.

10. Which of the following have been associated with the female sexual script?
    a. Sex is something women do for men.
    b. Men are more knowledgeable about what arouses women.
    c. A woman's sexual needs and pleasure are secondary to those of her partner.
    d. all of the above

11. A person who expresses feelings and is confident, aggressive, and caring could be described as:
    a. masculine.
    b. feminine.
    c. androgynous.
    d. homosexual.

12. Considerable evidence suggests that androgynous individuals and couples compared to sex-typed individuals and couples:
    a. have greater difficulty sustaining relationships and have lower self-esteem.
    b. tend to have greater confidence in social situations and a greater ability to form and sustain intimate relationships.
    c. have no differences in self-esteem or quality or quantity of relationships.
    d. have higher self-esteem but poorer ability to form and sustain intimate relationships.

13. Males or females processing ambiguous genitals are called:
    a. hermaphrodites.
    b. transsexuals.
    c. transgenderists.
    d. transvestites.

14. A chromosomal error affecting females who are born lacking an X chromosome is called:
    a. Klinefelter's syndrome.
    b. Turner's syndrome.
    c. transsexualism.
    d. pseudohermaphroditism.

15. Which of the following best defines the term "transsexual"?
    a. A person who is sexually aroused by wearing the clothing typical of the other sex
    b. A person who deeply feels incongruent with his or her sex and seeks surgery to achieve congruence
    c. A person who exaggerates the gender-typed behavior of the other sex
    d. A person who responds erotically to individuals of the same sex

Fill-In

Choose the correct term from the list at the end of this section.

1. Once a child's _____ is established, he or she will often react strongly if you call a boy a girl, or vice versa.

2. _____ is determined by chromosomes and hormones.

3. The collection of acts, rules, and expectations associated with the carrying out of a particular role is called a/an _____.

4. The theory that asserts that nature has structured us with an inborn desire to pass on our individual genes—and that this desire motivates much if not all of our behavior—is called _____.

5. According to cognitive social learning theory, boys and girls learn appropriate gender-role behavior through _____ by family and friends and by _____ or patterning their behavior after another.

6. According to Bem, the cognitive organization of the world according to gender is called gender _____.

7. Contemporary scripts, such as "both partners have a right to experience orgasm" or "sexual activities may be initiated by either partner" give increasing recognition to _____ sexuality.

8. _____ refers to flexibility in gender roles and the combination of masculine and feminine traits to reflect individual differences.

9. The state of dissatisfaction individuals experience when they feel they are trapped in the "wrong" sex is termed _____.

10. People who wish to have their genitals surgically altered to conform to their gender identity are known as _____.

anatomical sex	reinforcement
androgyny	schema
female	script
gender dysphoria	sociobiology
gender identity	transsexuals
modeling	

Matching

1. sex _____   a. The gender we feel ourselves to be

2. gender _____   b. Being biologically male or female based on genetic and anatomical sex

3. gender identity _____   c. A rigidly oversimplified belief that all males and females possess distinct psychological and behavioral traits

4. gender role _____   d. Masculinity or femininity; the social and cultural characteristics associated with our biological sex

5. gender-role stereotype _____   e. The beliefs we have of ourselves regarding appropriate male and female personality traits and activities

6. gender-role attitudes _____   f. The behavior that a person is expected to perform as a result of being male or female

Short Answer

1. According to gender theorists, how are gender differences created? Give examples of gender inequalities.

2. List three common traditional male and three female sexual scripts and briefly describe how each reinforces sex-role stereotypes.

3. List four ways that contemporary sexual scripts have changed for both sexes.

 **OBSERVATION**

Advertising Gender Stereotypes: Sexism in Toyland

As we grow up, we get many messages about being male and female from the toys and the products we play with and see. You can do this activity by going to a toy store, looking through a toy catalog, or watching TV ads aimed at children (try Saturday morning cartoon shows).

Fill in this chart to see what you learn.

Product	Gender (M, F, Both)	What made it seem gendered? (Activity, appearance, packaging, actors)	Comments

Did the products aimed at boys seem more action-oriented, mean, angry, or aggressive?
Did the products aimed at girls seem more passive, or show girls enjoying domestic tasks?
What percentage of toys were aimed at both genders?
What were the messages (either clear or subtle) about how boys or girls should act?

What did you learn by doing this assignment?

 **REFLECTION**

Advantages and Disadvantages of Being Male or Female

In the space below quickly brainstorm the advantages and disadvantages of being male and female.

Advantages of being female	**Disadvantages of being female**
Advantages of being male	**Disadvantages of being male**

After you complete the above, label each item either **P** (physical; innate or genetic) or **C** (cultural; learned or expected).

Which list is longer? Why?

If you have the time and would like to do so, share this activity with a friend, preferably of the other sex, and compare and discuss your lists. Often what one person sees as an advantage is seen as a disadvantage by another.

The next page has answers other students have given. Again note which are **P**hysical or **C**ultural.

Advantages of Being Female

usually doesn't pay for dates
live longer, hardier as infants
lower cardiovascular disease rate
greater variety in clothing selections
can and does show more emotion/feelings; cries
is the primary "nurturer"
can be "everything"—mother, wife, professional
it's acceptable to be a "little girl" or a "tomboy"
their arousal is more easily hidden (no embarrassing
    erections)
metabolizes and stores extra fat (warmth and
    softness)
don't have to shave their faces
no draft into the armed forces (yet)
less cultural pressure for job, money, education,
    or to be a success
acceptable to be fragile or physically weak (or
    pretend to be)
generally, have a closer relationship with their
    children than father
receives many cultural courtesies; i.e., car doors
    open, "ladies first," etc.
can use menstruation as an excuse to be bitchy,
    emotional, or irrational
may have the option to work or not to work
usually more intuitive

Advantages of Being Male

job superiority and higher pay
easier bathroom convenience, esp. outdoors
doesn't take long to dress
no shaving of legs/armpits
no periods & menstrual symptoms
no menopause
no pregnancy
natural to take aggressor role
almost always has an orgasm
no makeup
no birth control worries
"reputation" not at stake
variety of female partners as they become older
being breadwinner in family
body power, size
easier to detect STD
genitals prized, symbol of power and strength
    and superiority
less prone to weight problems
less sexual abuse (rape)
easier and cheaper to sterilize (vasectomy)
more freedom and independence as infant, child,
    teen, adult
fewer domestic responsibilities as child, teen, adult
can completely "retire" at 55
can age gracefully; looks "distinguished" with gray hair
braver, less fearful in dangerous or violent situations
can really relax when he comes home from work
can have expensive toys; i.e., cars, boats, motorcycles

Disadvantages of Being Female

period and premenstrual symptoms
harder to urinate, messier
pregnancy, labor, and delivery
weaker, smaller in size
makeup and dressing is more expensive
menopause
double standard of sexual conduct
job opportunities are less
weight watch—greater % of body fat
genitals thought to be ugly, shameful, dirty
household duties expected
must be "EVERYTHING"—mother, lover, friend, wife,
    professional, housewife, etc.
generally higher cost to groom, dress, and hygiene
shaving legs, armpits, etc.
usually has the full responsibility for birth control
generally unacceptable for her to be aggressive
often expected to "pay off" after a date
usually harder or taboo to initiate relationships
must be "lady-like"; no swearing
needs more time, romance, emotion, and intimacy with sex
breast and cervical cancers
greater longevity might mean being alone after spouse dies
alone and vulnerable after a divorce
STDs and their symptoms less visible, hidden in female body
unequal pay for equal jobs
her reputation is always at stake (double standard)
has to be extra cautious (worries) about going out alone
    at night
career interference by pregnancy/children (no job leave
    guarantees)
her fertility potential and marriageability limited by
    her age

Disadvantages of Being Male

pays for date
can't show emotions
shaves face
longer working hours or years
has to be initiator
has to put up with female mood changes
higher cardiovascular rate (diseases)
expected to be strong, leader, father breadwinner
expected to be macho/masculine to be accepted
can't have children or breastfeed
can't be feminine; play with dolls, do dishes, laundry,
    etc., without "criticism"
performance pressures (sexual and non-sexual)
the draft
expected to be the family disciplinarian "Mr. Bad Guy"
expected to be "Mr. Fixit": mechanic, electrician, plumber
can't hide arousal (tell-tale erections)
since he's usually the initiator, more subject to rejection
has difficulty with being physically warm, tender, or close
    in relationships; difficult to cry and show emotions,
    be intimate
often disciplined more severely
often judged by salary or status
custody battles, rarely gets custody of children, even if he
    wants them

Note: The authors thank Terry Frohoff for these sample lists

 **REFLECTION**

Gender Messages

Once again, try to recall the messages you received from your parents about being a boy or girl. Now imagine or recall the messages you might want to give to your children. What lessons would you repeat, and which would you change? Think in terms of appropriate behavior, clothing, chores, amount of freedom, messages about sex, extracurricular activities, and career guidance.

Messages you would repeat:

Messages you would not repeat:

Are these issues ones that you might choose to discuss with your partner before having children?

REFLECTION

Masculinity, Femininity, and Androgyny

Increased interest in androgynous gender roles has led to the development of a number of instruments to measure masculinity, femininity, and androgyny in individuals. The one below is patterned after the Bem Sex Role Inventory (BSRI), which is one of the most widely used tests (Bem, 1974, 1981).

To get a rough idea of how androgynous you are, examine the 21 personality traits below. Use a scale of 1 to 5 to indicate how well a personality trait describes you.

1	2	3	4	5
NOT AT ALL	SLIGHTLY	SOMEWHAT	QUITE A BIT	VERY MUCH

1. Aggressive	8. Shy	15. Moody
2. Understanding	9. Unsystematic	16. Dominating
3. Helpful	10. Strong	17. Warm
4. Decisive	11. Affectionate	18. Unpredictable
5. Nurturing	12. Cordial	19. Independent-minded
6. Happy	13. Assertive	20. Compassionate
7. Risk-taker	14. Tender	21. Reliable

Scoring

Your masculinity, femininity, and androgyny scores may be determined as follows:

1. To determine your masculinity score, add up your answers for numbers 1, 4, 7, 10, 13, 16, and 19, and divide the sum by seven.

2. To determine your femininity score, add up your answers for numbers 2, 5, 8, 11, 14, 17, and 20, and divide the sum by seven.

3. To determine your androgyny score, subtract the femininity score from the masculinity score.

The closer your score is to zero, the more androgynous you are. A high positive score indicates masculinity; a high negative score indicates femininity. A high masculine score not only indicates masculine attributes but also a rejection of feminine attributes. Similarly, a high feminine score indicates not only feminine characteristics, but a rejection of masculine attributes.

Source: Strong, Bryan, Christine DeVault, and Barbara Sayad. *The Marriage and Family Experience,* 7th ed., Belmont, CA: Wadsworth Publishing Company, 1998.

GENDER AND SEXUAL IDENTITY QUESTIONS

Gender Issues

This chapter, probably more than any other, directly and indirectly touches on key factors that affect your gender and sexual identity. A number of these issues will be addressed in other chapters. For the sake of brevity and in order to avoid duplication, we will address only those issues that are emphasized in this chapter.

- Since I was a boy/girl, my parents dressed me . . .

- I first recall feeling masculine/feminine when . . .

- My parents treated me because of/in spite of my gender by . . .

- My gender-role behavior has been most influenced by . . .

- They influenced me by . . .

- My feelings about my gender are . . .

- The gender identity I present to the world is . . .

- Concerning my gender-role behavior, I feel it works to my advantage when . . .

- Concerning my gender-role behavior, I feel limited when . . .

- I would like to change this by . . .

In our house, my parents were very loving, at least around me, and therefore my first impressions were that love is one of the most important things in life. Loving yourself as well as others can bring a lot more happiness when you are able to express your sexual self without embarrassment or awkwardness. Now that I look back on it, my parents were more open than most in expressing what they felt was appropriate. Not only that, they were understanding and reassuring when it came to sexual questions and behavior.

—27-year-old Caucasian female

Throughout my life, I have related much closer to guys that I have to girls. Being the oldest child, and needing to be responsible, I was much closer to my father and therefore I was more of a "tomboy" than most of the girls. I played softball, rode dirt bikes, played Army, and hung out with the boys all of my life. Even with this strong sense of being a tomboy, my identity as a female remained intact. I just felt that I was a girl having more fun playing boy games. Through having so many male friends I developed a better understanding of males and an understanding of how they thought about females. After starting high school, these male friendships began to change. I began dating on a more serious level, and I was not always considered one of the guys anymore.

—20-year-old Caucasian female

I am not the totally masculine man, and as such, I can react with warmth and compassion and not be afraid to do "woman's work." I display the best human traits possible, whether the characteristics are considered masculine or feminine.

—35-year-old African male

My father, being Mexican, taught me how to be the typical Latin, macho man. He would tell me that "to be a man" you had to be strong and never show any weakness. I was taught not to cry, to defend what was mine, to be a provider, and other similar messages. My mother, on the other hand, taught me to be a warm and sensitive person. She told me that a woman was to be treated like a rose, delicate and with respect. Needless to say, I was rather confused on how to treat women.

—20-year-old Hispanic male

9. Children who are curious about sex and who masturbate:
   a. are normal.
   b. need psychological counseling.
   c. need to be told that this is "bad" behavior.
   d. probably are not getting normal affection from their parents.

10. Lesbians:
   a. have virtually no ties with the gay male community.
   b. tend to value the emotional quality of relationships more than the sexual components.
   c. form shorter-lasting relationships than gay males.
   d. disdain the idea of parenthood and family.

11. Cohabitation:
   a. significantly increases the chance for later marital stability.
   b. significantly decreases the chance for later marital stability.
   c. has not proven to significantly increase or decrease the chance for marital stability.
   d. increases for women but decreases for men the chance for later marital stability.

12. One important difference that exists between heterosexual and gay and lesbian couples is that:
   a. gay and lesbian couples are less committed than heterosexual couples.
   b. gay and lesbian couples tend to have "best-friend" or egalitarian relationships.
   c. heterosexual couples emphasize love and are more romantic than lesbian or gay couples.
   d. heterosexual couples are naturally inclined to settle down and start a family, whereas gay and lesbian ones are not.

13. Helene lived with Jim for two years beginning at age 19. When she was 24, she and Bill married. A few years after their divorce, at age 32, she began living with Michael and they plan to marry. Helene's way of life is best described as
   a. serial monogamy.
   b. confused.
   c. intermittent cohabitation.
   d. promiscuity.

14. The most significant factors affecting sexuality in older adults are:
   a. diffusion of sexual feelings and decrease in physical attractiveness.
   b. decrease in physical attractiveness and disinterest in sex.
   c. health and partner availability.
   d. inability of men to have erections and stereotypes about sex and the elderly.

True/False

_____ 1. An important and normal aspect of child psychosexual development is the need for privacy.

_____ 2. Young people first learn about communication and gender roles when they reach adolescence.

_____ 3. Many, perhaps most, children who participate in sex play do so with a member of their same sex.

_____ 4. During adolescence, young people are often too embarrassed to ask their parents about their sexuality and, at the same time, parents are too ambivalent about their children's developing sexual nature.

_____ 5. Gay and lesbian adolescents usually have heterosexual dating experiences during their teens but they report ambivalent feelings about them.

_____ 6. Most people who have sexual experiences with both sexes identify themselves as bisexual.

_____ 7. When it comes to household tasks and responsibilities, cohabitating couples adhere to traditional gender roles as much as married couples do.

_____ 8. Scholars suggest that divorce does not represent a devaluation of marriage, but an idealization of it.

_____ 9. The United States leads the world's developed nations in teen pregnancies.

_____ 10. Most married couples feel that declining frequency of sex is a major problem in their relationship.

Fill-In

1. The authors point to research that stresses that children's sexual exploration or activities should never be

    labeled as "bad" but that they may be called _____.

2. The physical changes of puberty are centered around the onset of _____ in girls and

    _____ in boys.

3. The biological stage when reproduction becomes possible is called _____.

4. The psychological state of _____ is a time of growth and often confusion, as the body matures faster than the emotional and intellectual abilities.

5. The changes that occur in the psychological aspects of sexuality as a child grows are referred to as that

    child's _____ development.

6. _____ refers to relationships in which self-esteem and status are linked to evaluations from people of the same sex.

7. _____ refers to relationships with the other sex that are based on respect and friendship.

8. The term used to refer to the sexual activities that occur primarily among unmarried, divorced, or

    widowed adults is _____ sex.

9. _____ sex refers to sexual activities, especially sexual intercourse, that take place prior to marriage.

10. Consensual extramarital sex in which couples engage in sexual relations with others is called

    _____.

11. Married partners who may mutually agree to allow sexual relationships with others have what is called a/an

    _____.

adolescence	nonmarital
ejaculation	open marriage
heterosociality	premarital
homosociality	psychosexual
inappropriate	puberty
menstruation	swinging

Short Answer

1. Briefly describe how, according to the authors, the experience of self-stimulation should be addressed with children.

2. Discuss three factors that contribute to the low rate of contraceptive use among teenagers.

3. Briefly describe the multifaceted approach to reducing teen pregnancy.

4. Cite two factors that have influenced attitudes and made premarital intercourse more acceptable.

5. Living together has become more widespread and acceptable. Cite two advantages and two disadvantages to cohabiting.

 **OBSERVATION**

The School Board Is Called to Order

Imagine that you are a member of the local school board, and the issue has been raised about whether condoms should be distributed in your local high school. Tonight at the meeting they are going to be asking for your view on the subject. Do you feel they should be available and, if so, how should they be distributed? Write out what you will state as your position and how you will defend it.

There is also a discussion at the meeting about at what age AIDS education should begin and how explicit it should be at each grade level. Parents are raising objections because they don't want discussions of homosexuality, anal sex, and oral sex included in the schools. Others feel that it is necessary to give proper education on these subjects.

What are you going to state as your general position on these issues?

At what grade level do you think these issues need to be discussed? Make an X in those grades where you think it should be taught. You can mark more than one grade for each subject. Ask two other people and use O and Δ to show their answers.

Subject	Early Elementary (K–3)	Late Elementary (4–6)	Middle School (7–8)	High School (9–12)	Should Not Be Discussed in School
AIDS					
Other STDs					
Homosexuality					
Condoms					
Anal Sex					
Oral Sex					
Masturbation					
Injectable Drugs					

Did everyone agree with the grade levels?

What issues were there differences on?

What reasons did others give for their choices?

REFLECTION

Answering Questions About Sex in the Tender Years

Consider the following scenarios. How might you react in each situation? Someday you may have to deal with similar situations.

1. Your 6-year-old daughter enjoys masturbating regardless of where she might be.

2. Your 3-year-old son and his 4-year-old boyfriend are "caught" by you while playing doctor.

3. Your 8-year-old son asks you what "sex" is.

4. Your 15-year-old son asks you for money to buy condoms.

5. Your 15-year-old daughter asks you for money to buy condoms.

How might your parents have responded to these situations? How do your responses differ from theirs?

If you are comfortable, share these responses with someone close to you. How do they differ? How are they similar?

 **OBSERVATION**

Dating Customs

Dating is a relatively new phenomenon that is practiced mainly in Western countries. Observers of dating have noticed ongoing changes and differences across social, racial, and ethnic lines.

Interview at least one or two acquaintances (preferably from another generation and/or social, racial, or ethnic group) to see how others regard dating. Compare their experiences and attitudes to your own. Feel free to add or delete any questions you desire.

1. What are your first memories of dating?

2. At what age were you allowed to date?

3. What type of dating did you first participate in? (just one couple, in groups, with chaperones, etc.)

4. What types of activities or places were part of your first few dates?

5. Did your religion give you messages about dating?
   Was it encouraged/discouraged?

6. Did your schooling give you messages about dating?

   Was it encouraged/discouraged?

7. Did your parents give you messages about dating?
   Was it encouraged/discouraged?

8. What physical activities were a part of dating, and at what stage of dating did they occur?
   Holding hands?
   Arms around the other person?
   Kissing?
   Intimate touching?

As a result of these interviews what did you learn? How did others' experiences and attitudes about dating differ from your own?

Adapted from Maxine Baca Zinn and D. Stanley Eitzin, *Diversity in Families,* 2d ed. (New York: Harper & Row, 1990).

 **REFLECTION**

Attitudes Toward Aging and Sex

Please respond to the following statements:

1. Older people are sexual people.

2. Most older women and men enjoy intercourse and/or masturbation.

3. Menopause is normal and natural and does not necessarily interfere with the expression of a woman's sexuality.

4. Nursing homes and residential care facilities should respect the privacy of older adults who wish to express their sexuality.

Look at your responses. Are your attitudes about sexuality and the aged accepting or not? How do you think your attitudes about older adults will impact your behavior when you are aged?

REFLECTION

Placing Relationships into Life's Continuum

Below is a continuum. On the far left is your birth (day 1) and on the far right is the number of years you believe you might live.

Day 1   **Age at Death**

|———|

Take some time to explore the significant life events that you anticipate. At what age do you expect each to occur? Fill out the continuum by drawing a small line relative to where you believe certain events will occur and briefly describe them. These can include:

- Graduate from high school

- Graduate from college

- Cite all the degrees you anticipate earning at the age you will obtain them

- First career job; retirement from that job

- Second or third career

- Marriage or significant relationship(s)

- Children; how many and how far apart

- Hobbies and travel

- Other

Now look at the whole continuum. Where are most events clustered? What do you have listed at the last one-third of your continuum? How do you feel about this time of your life? What are you doing now to plan for that time?

Think about your relationship and partner. Do you see yourself as being committed in a long-term relationship? Can you imagine yourself being sexual throughout your life? What attitudes do you have or can you begin to cultivate now to better prepare you for your later years as a sexual person?

GENDER AND SEXUAL IDENTITY QUESTIONS

Early Childhood Sexuality

Because a large part of who we are and how we feel comes from experiences and observations that occurred during our childhood and adolescence, more questions appear in this section than in others. Take time to fill out the questions below, perhaps responding to them over a few days time. Don't feel limited to the questions or the format in which they are presented.

- When I was a little girl/boy, my parents dressed me . . .

- The toys they gave me included . . .

- I was taught to be . . .

- I first recall being curious about the opposite sex when I was about _____ years old.

- My curiosity was satisfied when . . .

  (I was not curious and/or my curiosity was not satisfied.)

- I began to masturbate when I was _____ years old.

- I recall feeling . . .

- My parents' attitudes about my masturbating was . . .

- Nudity in my family was . . .

- My feelings about my sexual maturation were . . .

- My parents acknowledged my sexual maturation by . . .

- Concerning my sex education, my parents told me . . .

- These conversations occurred . . .

- I feel the impact of the sex education my parents gave me on my sexuality has been . . .
  because . . .

- During my adolescence, my friends and associates influenced me by . . .

- My sexual orientation became apparent to me when I was about _____.
  This was a result of . . .

- My first sexual experience (which does not have to include sexual intercourse) with someone I was
  attracted to occurred . . .

- Concerning this experience I felt . . .

- The most positive aspect of my adolescence was . . .

- The most negative aspect of my adolescence was . . .

- From my earlier experiences I feel . . .

A good friend of mine and I (both 10 years old at the time) hung around each other all the time. We were so close to each other that we would sleep over at each other's house and after everybody would go to bed we would stay up and examine each other and touch each other's penis and watch it get hard.

—27-year-old Caucasian male

I was in first grade and had received all "S" and "E"'s on my report card; I was sure to get what I asked for. Fidgeting in my dress, it was finally my turn to sit on Santa's lap. He looked at me and said, "So, little girl, what dolly can Santa bring you this year?" I earnestly replied, "I don't like dollys. I want a Super Cliffhanger Racing Tyco Glow-in-the-Dark Race and Track Set!!!" Santa began to argue with me. He told me that little girls don't play with cars, and that pretty little girls were supposed to play with dolls. I jumped off of Santa's lap and turned around and looked him straight in the eye and said, "I have 181 hot wheels, more than any other boy on my block.... Don't you remember me, Santa?" That Christmas, I got my Super Cliffhanger Racing Tyco Glow-in-the-Dark Race and Track Set. It appears I got my point through to Santa Claus loud and clear.

—20-year-old Caucasian female

I clearly remember the day my first menstruation began. At first I thought I had a stomach ache as I experienced a strong pain in my abdomen. But when I saw the bleeding, I got scared. I did not understand what was happening to me. I could not tell my mother about it since the subject of sexuality was never discussed in our family. What I did to let her know that something was happening to me was to not flush the toilet. As soon as my mother saw it, she came to me, but just to calmly say that I needed a sanitary pad. She did not say word about what was happening to me. I felt very scared and confused.

—23-year-old Hispanic female

In junior high, I found myself still very curious about other boys and what they were like. I found myself attracted to some of them, but rationalized that it was a phase, and I was just curious and wanted to see what their bodies looked like. I kept telling myself that I was just a late bloomer and that I would start liking girls soon. I found that I was telling myself this throughout my entire four years in high school. Any day I would find the girl who would catch my attention (the truth was that I was still looking at other guys but hoping against hope that this was still a phase, albeit a long one).

—24-year-old Caucasian gay male

I thought I had "escaped" the scars and trauma of my parents' divorce and considered myself lucky they had divorced when I was so young. In retrospect I have learned that the divorce did have a great impact on the development of my sexual identity. Not having a father take an active role in my life gave me a feeling of rejection I did not understand until just recently. I realized that I have developed many close personal friendships with the young men with whom I associate. I am reassured by their friendship and trust that I am appreciated by men even though I felt rejection from my father.

—25-year-old Caucasian female whose parents divorced when she was two

My wife and I are very comfortable with our sexuality. We have a very open line of communication. This line of communication is what allows us to have the type of relationship we share: swinging.... We knew early on in the relationship that we were both different. We dated a long time before we ever had sex, and that was unheard of for me. Back then in our relationship, it was pretty much conventional. Oh, we liked to do different things, but there were no other people involved yet. After a year and a half of dating, we were married. I was 20 and she was 18; we were just kids.... I wanted adventure, and I damn well knew I didn't want a white bread type of life. Many people from this area saw this period of my life as my downfall, but I see it as Karen's and my rebirth. Away from this area, Karen felt open about her bisexuality and fully embraced it.... We began to share partners and we found it to be most rewarding. We found new heights of sexuality. It wasn't that our relationship was lacking anything, because we had all the elements of a great relationship. It was as if this lifestyle complements our relationship rather than replacing something or adding a missing element. If anything, we feel as if it strengthens our relationship.

—28-year-old Caucasian male.

CHAPTER 7
LOVE, INTIMACY, AND SEXUALITY

LEARNING OBJECTIVES

At the conclusion of Chapter 7, students should be able to:

1. Discuss similarities and differences in attitudes toward love by heterosexual men and women and by gay men and lesbians.

2. Discuss sex without emotional attachment and celibacy as a choice.

3. Identify the attitudes and behaviors associated with love.

4. List, describe, and give examples of the different styles of love.

5. List the components of the triangular theory of love and describe how they combine to create different forms of love.

6. Discuss love as a form of attachment, including the different styles of attachment.

7. Discuss the relationship between friendship and love.

8. Discuss jealousy, including psychological dimensions, types of jealousy, and jealousy as a boundary marker.

9. Discuss the roles of commitment, caring, and self-disclosure in intimate love.

10. Recognize and define the key terms listed below.

Key Terms

celibacy
eros
mania
ludus
storge
agape
pragma
triangular theory of love
attachment
jealousy

suspicious jealousy
reactive jealousy
commitment
caring
self-disclosure
secure attachment
anxious/ambivalent attachment
avoidant attachment
deception

PRACTICE TEST QUESTIONS

(For answers see Part IV of this book.)

Multiple Choice

1. Which one of the following statements about the study of love is accurate?
    a. Psychologists have been involved in researching the nature of love since the founding days of the discipline.
    b. When there is real love between two people, it smooths over all differences.
    c. The dark side of love is anger and frustration.
    d. Love refers to both a subjective feeling and overt behaviors.

2. Men are *more likely* than women to:
    a. separate sex and love.
    b. find sex and love incompatible.
    c. prefer sexual experiences that take place in a relational context.
    d. experience jealousy over intimacy issues.

3. Women:
    a. are more likely to report feelings of love if they are sexually involved with their partners.
    b. report that love is closely related to feelings of self-esteem.
    c. generally view sex from a relational perspective.
    d. all of the above

4. Which statement best reflects the core idea of attachment theory?
    a. For a love relationship to endure, there must be a balance among love, commitment, and passion.
    b. Feelings of love are due to physiological arousal and labeling that feeling as love.
    c. One can distinguish among six types of love.
    d. Adult love relationships replicate the qualities of the infant/caregiver bond.

5. Nina and Bart have known each other since high school. After many years of marriage, they divorce. Nonetheless, they continue to be involved in each other's lives and rely on each other in times of need. This relationship is an example of which type of love?
    a. Agape
    b. Pragma
    c. Storge
    d. Eros

6. If we can understand jealousy we can:
    a. eliminate some of its pain.
    b. see when and how it is functional and when it is not.
    c. recognize its link with violence.
    d. all of the above

7. The potential for jealousy is increased when there is a perceived lack of:
    a. independence.
    b. self-esteem.
    c. humor.
    d. a and b only

8. The most intense kind of jealousy is:
    a. suspicious jealousy.
    b. manic jealousy.
    c. reactive jealousy.
    d. depressive jealousy.

9. Which of the following is NOT one of Sternberg's components of the triangular theory of love?
   a. intimacy
   b. commitment
   c. passion
   d. companionate

10. When Vicky tells her boyfriend she has to work late, he "surprises" her by bringing dinner to her office. When she leaves town to visit a seriously ill relative, he calls her almost every hour to ask who else is there. This boyfriend may be experiencing _____ jealousy.
    a. suspicious
    b. storgic
    c. reactive
    d. defensive

11. The kind of love that is most likely to sustain over a period of time is:
    a. intimate love.
    b. passionate love.
    c. romantic love.
    d. complex love.

12. After many years of living together, Anne and Jim are really the closest of friends and confidantes. They love traveling together and are involved in each other's careers. Both express high satisfaction with this. They often hold hands, hug, and kiss. This kind of love is most accurately described as
    a. fatuous love.
    b. companionate love.
    c. consummate love.
    d. liking.

13. Models of how people define love and sex are called:
    a. prototypes.
    b. morals.
    c. attachments.
    d. values.

14. All of the following statements are true about deception EXCEPT:
    a. It erodes bonds and blocks authentic communication.
    b. It is extremely rare in intimate relationships.
    c. It typically originates with betrayal or lies.
    d. It leaves a couple operating on a higher level of anxiety.

15. All of the following typify "intimate love" (or liking) EXCEPT:
    a. being able to count on each other.
    b. excitement from achievement of other life goals.
    c. romantic feelings.
    d. continued caring.

Fill-In

Choose the correct term from the list at the end of this section.

1. The models or ideas that we carry around in our minds regarding the elements of love and sex are called

   _____.

2. _____ jealousy usually occurs when one member of a couple feels ignored in favor of someone else when there is no evidence to support the feeling.

3. The determination to continue in a relationship, based on conscious choice rather than on feelings and on a promise of a shared future, is called _____.

4. The type of love that idealizes its object, is marked by a high degree of physical and emotional arousal, and tends to be obsessive and all-consuming is known as _____.

5. The type of love that combines intimacy and passion, begins with friendship that intensifies with passion, and may or may not include commitment is _____.

6. The newest approach to the study of love that involves a close, enduring emotional bond that finds its roots in infancy is called _____.

7. The type of jealousy that occurs when a partner reveals a current, past, or anticipated relationship with another person is called _____.

8. The revelation of information not normally known because of its riskiness is called: _____.

9. Making another's needs as important as your own is called _____.

10. An aversive response caused by a partner's real, imagined, or likely involvement with a third person is called

    _____.

attachment	prototypes
caring	reactive
commitment	romantic love
infatuation	self-disclosure
jealousy	suspicious

Matching

Match the description with the style of love, as described by the sociologist John Lee:

1. Eros _____
2. Mania _____
3. Ludus _____
4. Storge _____
5. Agape _____
6. Pragma _____

a. companionate love
b. altruistic love
c. love of beauty
d. practical love
e. playful love
f. obsessive love

Short Answer

1. Regardless of their sexual orientation, how are men and women different in terms of their attitudes toward love and sex?

2. Describe Sternberg's triangular theory of love.

3. Describe the differences that exist between reactive jealousy and suspicious jealousy.

REFLECTION AND OBSERVATION

The following two activities utilize Sternberg's triangle of love and Lee's basic styles of love to examine love and relationships. "Looking at Your Love Patterns" takes a personal approach toward this objective while "Looking At Love on the Radio and in the Movies" examines music and media. Pick the approach that you wish to explore further and respond to the questions and statements listed in that activity.

Looking at Your Love Patterns

The textbook presented two theoretical ideas about love that you may wish to use when evaluating relationships, especially those that have involved love.

BASIC STYLES OF LOVE—The sociologist John Lee describes six basic styles of love and provides brief descriptions of each. For a more detailed description of the chart below, look on page 208 of the textbook. Which types of love have you experienced? With whom? Which type have you found the most satisfying? Why? (Remember, the same relationship can go through several styles.)

Eros	*Mania*	*Ludus*	*Storge*	*Agape*	*Pragma*
Beauty	Obsessive	Playful	Companionate	Altruistic	Practical

YOUR LOVE TRIANGLE—Robert Sternberg's triangular theory of love is shown in the diagram in Figure 2 on page 213. Using this theory as a guide, think about a relationship you have been in, or one you know well, and draw the triangle to represent the Intimacy, Passion, and Decision/Commitment levels. Draw one triangle for each partner. If you are in a relationship, you might explain this concept to your partner and ask him or her to draw a triangle representing how he or she sees these three elements in your relationship. You can use the list below to further define your relationship. (Remember, the same relationship can go through several stages.)

Liking: intimacy only
Infatuation: passion only
Romantic love: intimacy and passion
Companionate love: intimacy and commitment

Fatuous love: passion and commitment
Consummate love: intimacy, passion, and commitment
Empty love: decision or commitment only
Nonlove: no intimacy, passion, or commitment

Are there any ways to help these three important aspects of your relationship become stronger? Does reflecting on the diagrams give some insight into the weaknesses or strengths of the relationship? Keep and refer back to these diagrams to see if there are changes you notice in the relationship.

Looking at Love on the Radio and in the Movies

Turn on your radio, find a station that has songs (with lyrics) that suit your style and, for the next half hour or so, listen to the messages that love songs give about love. What kinds of love do the songs describe? See if you can apply Lee's work on "Style of Love" by making a check under the proper category.

Song Title	*Eros* Beauty	*Mania* Obsessive	*Ludus* Playful	*Storge* Companionate	*Agape* Altruistic	*Pragma* Practical

Did you find a trend in the type of love that was sung about?

Think of a recent movie or novel that showed details of a relationship. Using Sternberg's "Triangle Theory of Love," classify the type or types of love demonstrated. Remember that as relationships progress they may go through several stages.

Liking: intimacy only
Infatuation: passion only
Romantic love: intimacy and passion
Companionate love: intimacy and commitment

Fatuous love: passion and commitment
Consummate love: intimacy, passion, and commitment
Empty love: decision or commitment only
Nonlove: no intimacy, passion, or commitment

Movie or novel title	*Type of Relationship* (from the list above)	*Justify your classification*

 **OBSERVATION**

Looking at Cohabitation

Does cohabiting before marriage increase the success and improve the quality of a marriage? Not necessarily. The most notable social impact of cohabitation is that it delays the age of marriage for those who live together. As a consequence, cohabitation may actually encourage more stable marriages because the older a person is at the time of marriage, the less likely he or she is to divorce. Still there is no consensus on whether cohabitation significantly increases or decreases later marital stability, as such couples are statistically as likely to divorce as those who do not live together before marriage.

How does the above information compare with your own and others' thoughts and observations about cohabiting? To find out, interview several couples or divorced individuals, some of whom cohabited before marriage and some of whom did not. Ask them the following questions:

1. Did you live together before getting married?

2. How long did you live together before you got married?

3. What prompted you to get married?

4. How would you rate the quality of your marriage?

5. Do you feel that living together increased, decreased, or had no effect on the quality of your marriage?

6. Would you recommend living together?

7. Brainstorm the advantages and disadvantages of living together before marriage. Based on this list and your feelings about the subject, which lifestyle (living together before marriage or not) would you choose? Why?

REFLECTION

Vows and Prenuptial Agreements

1. There are some who feel that a "prenuptial agreement" or contract is an important component to consider before marriage. Assuming you are one of these individuals, what might you include in yours? (You may wish to include division of household tasks, baby-sitting arrangements, career decisions, pets, relations with in-laws and friends, and discussions about religion.)

2. This activity is done best when you have 15 or 20 minutes alone to reflect on what marriage means to you. Compose your marriage vows. This should be an accurate reflection of how you perceive marriage to be. Hold onto this list and reflect back upon it from time to time. If you are married, how closely does your marriage match these vows? Why or why not?

As a result of this exercise, what did you learn about your expectations of marriage?

 **OBSERVATION**

Looking at Love

Interview one or two people who are in a long-term (at least two years), committed relationship. Ask them how they knew when they were "in love." Find out if their level of intimacy has changed over time. Ask them the differences between being "in love" versus being "in infatuation" with another. Ask them what qualities contribute to a successful relationship. Depending on how well you know the person, and keeping in mind that the following are more sensitive issues, inquire about how cross-cultural perspectives, jealousy, and gender differences are handled within the relationship.

Following the interview, state what you learned. How do the other person's perspectives and experiences compare with those that you have observed or experienced?

GENDER AND SEXUAL IDENTITY QUESTIONS

Experiences of Love

- I have/have not been in love.
    This first happened when . . .

- The most profound type of love I ever experienced was with _____. I felt . . .

- As a result of that love, I learned . . .

- The most satisfying type of love for me is _____ because . . .

- Probably the most painful experience I have had as a result of love was . . .

- I experienced or observed jealousy when. . .

- My experience of love has affected my sexual identity by . . .

During my early teen years, my budding sexuality was motivated by rebellion against my grandmother, her emotional abuse, and denial of sexuality as a normal and healthy expression of one's identity. My rebellion took the form of sexual promiscuity by the time I had become 14 years old. Sex became a means of both defying my grandmother and obtaining love and closeness, if only for a little while.

—39-year-old Caucasian female

People would perceive me as self-assured, independent, confident, and secure, and in many areas I am all of those things. That doesn't mean a lot though, if you can't be free to love and be loved.

—27-year-old Caucasian female

I was away from home for the very first time and got caught up in the college scene. I had my very first sexual experience in my first year of college on my eighteenth birthday. It was with someone I had just met that night at a party. I knew very well what I wanted to do that night. I was getting tired of being sexually naive except for information I got from other people's experiences. I was very disappointed after that experience because I did not have fun, and I never really saw that guy again. There was no emotion. After that experience, I thought every sexual experience was supposed to be uncomfortable. I felt I had to give in to the guy's passes and have sex with him the very first night or within the first few weeks. Thank goodness it did not take very many experiences like that to knock some sense into me about what a relationship should be. When I realized that a relationship need not be emotionless and uncaring, I stopped all sexual activity until I was sure that I was interested in the person beyond just one night.

—26-year-old Caucasian female

CHAPTER 8
COMMUNICATING ABOUT SEX

LEARNING OBJECTIVES

At the conclusion of Chapter 8, students should be able to:

1. Discuss the cultural, social, and psychological contexts of communication with examples of each.

2. Identify the role of proximity, eye contact, and touching in nonverbal communication.

3. Describe communication in beginning and established relationships, including the halo effect, interest and opening lines, the first move, initiating and directing sexual activity, and gay and lesbian relationships.

4. Discuss "safer sex" including disclosure of lifestyle and STD information to potential partners.

5. List and give examples of communication patterns in satisfied relationships and discuss gender differences in marital communication.

6. Discuss the obstacles and problems with sexual vocabulary in talking about sex.

7. Describe and give examples of the keys to good sexual communication, including self-disclosure, trust, and feedback.

8. List the guidelines for effective feedback with examples of each.

9. Discuss types of conflicts and the nature and sources of power in intimate relationships, including the power of love.

10. Describe sexual conflicts, including sex and power issues, the characteristics of conflict resolution in happy and unhappy couples, and strategies for resolving conflicts.

11. Recognize and define the key terms listed below.

Key Terms

communication	halo effect	feedback
status	self-disclosure	conflict
proximity	trust	

PRACTICE TEST QUESTIONS

(For answers see Part IV of this book.)

Multiple Choice

1. Why is it important to improve communication about sex in a relationship?
    a. Good sexual communication can transform a bad relationship into a good one.
    b. Good sexual communication can turn an indifferent or angry partner into a loving and considerate one.
    c. Good sex can lead to good communication and vice versa.
    d. Couples satisfied with their sexual communication express greater relationship satisfaction.

2. The indirectness and reliance on nonverbal communication among Asian Americans serve to maintain the cultural norm of:
    a. individual self-expression.
    b. valuing experiential knowledge and emotional expressiveness.
    c. deep intimacy between spouses and direct confrontation about emotional issues.
    d. valuing harmony and the avoidance of conflict.

3. In order to talk openly about sexual matters, it is often important for a couple to:
   a. negotiate about the language that will be used.
   b. acknowledge that they both have dirty minds and prurient interests.
   c. begin with difficult topics such as interest in sadomasochism, erotic fantasies, etc. This will increase trust.
   d. understand that they will be rusking their relationship.

4. If Tamika is interested in that man looking at her from across the room, she can communicate this by
   a. quickly lowering her gaze.
   b. looking around the room, and not stopping at other men.
   c. prolonging eye contact with him, for just a few seconds.
   d. folding her arms over her chest.

5. Touch:
   a. often signals intimacy, immediacy, and emotional closeness.
   b. is initiated by men equally as often as by women.
   c. appears to be linked to self-disclosure.
   d. all of the above

6. In new or developing relationships, communication about sexuality is generally:
   a. direct and straightforward.
   b. indirect and ambiguous.
   c. non-existent.
   d. unimportant.

7. The sense most involved in sexual intimacy is:
   a. sight.
   b. sound.
   c. touch.
   d. smell.

8. In established relationships between men and women, many women feel more comfortable with overtly initiating sex because:
   a. of the decreasing significance of the double standard.
   b. it may be viewed as an expression of love.
   c. it can be the result of couples becoming more egalitarian in their gender-role attitudes.
   d. all of the above

9. One of the key differences between heterosexual couples and gay couples is:
   a. how they handle extrarelational sex.
   b. their enjoyment of sex.
   c. who initiates sex.
   d. the type of communication that is expressed prior to having sex.

10. Which of the following is/are true regarding marital communication?
   a. Wives send clearer messages to their husbands than their husbands send to them.
   b. Husbands, more than wives, tend to give neutral messages.
   c. Wives tend to set the emotional tone of an argument.
   d. all of the above

11. The least successful way to resolve conflict is to:
   a. agree as a gift.
   b. bargain.
   c. give in.
   d. coexist.

True/False

Mark T or F on the line before the statement.

_____ 1. Couples who are satisfied with their sexual communication are generally more satisfied with their overall relationship.

_____ 2. Despite stereotypes of women touching and men avoiding touch, studies suggest that there are no consistent differences between the sexes in the amount of overall touching.

_____ 3. Any communication can be accurately interpreted by understanding the words.

_____ 4. The majority of people begin their sexual involvement in the context of an ongoing relationship.

_____ 5. Because so much of our sexual communication is direct, unambiguous, and verbal, there is little risk of misinterpretation between men and women.

_____ 6. Within established relationships, men continue to overtly initiate sexual encounters more frequently than women.

_____ 7. Researches have found that men and women in satisfied relationships are willing to engage in conflict in nondestructive ways.

_____ 8. The process of articulating our feelings about sex is usually quite easy because of the positive models that most children have grown up with.

_____ 9. One of the keys to good communication is to avoid self-disclosure because it creates an environment of misunderstanding.

_____ 10. The most crucial variable in explaining the power structure of a relationship is the degree to which one spouse loves and needs the other.

Fill-In

Choose the correct term from the list at the end of this section.

1. The thread that connects sexuality and intimacy is _____.

2. The revelation of intimate information about ourselves is called _____.

3. For a message to be most effective, both the verbal and nonverbal components must be in

   _____.

4. Nearness in physical space and time, such as where we sit or stand in relation to another person, is called

   _____.

5. The assumption that attractive people possess more desirable social characteristics than unattractive people is

   otherwise known as the _____.

6. An important first step in attempting to talk openly about sex is negotiating or agreeing on the

   _____ to be used.

7. A constructive response to another's self-disclosure is called _____.

8. The belief in the reliability and integrity of a person is known as _____.

9. A person's position in his or her social group is called _____.

10. The idea that the partner with the least investment in continuing a relationship has the most power is called the _____.

11. _____ is the ability or potential ability to influence another person or group.

12. The theory that explains power in terms of involvement and needs in a relationship is called _____ theory.

agreement	proximity
communication	relative love and need
feedback	self-disclosure
halo effect	status
power	trust
principle of least interest	vocabulary

Short Answer

1. Describe the functions of conveying interpersonal attitudes, expressing emotions, and handling the ongoing interaction in close relationships.

2. Discuss three reasons why misinterpretation of sexual communication can occur between women and men.

3. List and discuss two strategies for resolving conflicts within relationships.

 **OBSERVATION**

Games Singles Play

The purpose of this activity is to observe people communicating in a setting in which they feel comfortable. Choose a setting to visit that involves or caters to single people, such as a bar, community event (watch newspaper ads), or apartment complex pool or recreation area. (Single people were chosen because you can observe them engaging in a wide range of both verbal and nonverbal communication in their desire to get to know one another.)

While at the site, take a seat away from people and watch their body language. What gestures are used to communicate? How close do people sit next to one another? Can you differentiate those whose relationship is established from those who are newly acquainted? Observe the level of eye contact, posing, and touching that occurs. Who appears to be the more aggressive? What else do you notice about body language that helps to communicate interest or desire?

REFLECTION

Language and Sexuality

There are many reasons why people are uncomfortable talking about sex, including personal anxieties and cultural factors. Another factor is that they don't have a "language" they feel comfortable using to discuss sexual issues and feelings. Paul Cashman, Ph.D., has suggested that we have four "language systems" to use when we talk about sexuality. They are:

1. *Child language.* These are the words used by our parents when we were very young—often related to toilet training. Words like *wienie, bottom, tushy, pee-pee,* and *poo-poo* are examples of these types of words.

2. *Slang or street language.* This category probably has the greatest number of words. Often this is the way we talk about sex with our peers, and these are the words we see in graffiti in bathrooms. Words like *cock* and *cunt* are examples of street language.

3. *Euphemisms.* These are the words that allow us to talk about sex in "polite" conversations and relate to our Victorian heritage. Words like *making love, that time of month,* and *in the family way* are examples of euphemisms.

4. *Medical-scientific language.* We learn from school, books, and others that there is a technical language often used by professionals or parents to talk about sexuality. Words like *intercourse, coitus interruptus, penis,* and *menstruation* are examples of this type of language.

For each category write down some of the words that you have used or might use to talk about sex:

CHILD LANGUAGE

SLANG OR STREET LANGUAGE

EUPHEMISMS

MEDICAL-SCIENTIFIC LANGUAGE

Now answer the questions on the next page.

For which category was it easiest to list words?

For which groups was it hardest to think of words?

Which words do you think would be recognized by most others, and which are limited to family, partner, or a particular culture?

Which types of words are you most comfortable with?

Do you find the words you use change according to the situation or the person you are with? Why?

Each of us needs to think about what type of language we are comfortable using in different situations. There is nothing wrong with using child language in your intimate relationships, or street language if you or your partner find it exciting. What is important is finding words and ways to discuss sexual issues in a comfortable way. Whereas a great deal of sexual communication is nonverbal, the more words we have, the more precise and accurate we can be in communicating with others.

Note: The article cited is from SEICUS Reports, September 1980.

REFLECTION

Sexual Communication Satisfaction Questionnaire

This questionnaire assesses your satisfaction with your sexual communication with your partner. Use the following scale below to indicate how strongly you agree or disagree with each statement. You may want to ask your partner to give his or her answers and compare your responses. Are you satisfied with the quality of communication in your relationship? If not, is there anything you and your partner can do to improve it?

1 = Strongly agree   4 = Disagree
2 = Agree   5 = Strongly disagree
3 = Neither agree nor disagree

_____ 1. I find it difficult to talk about sexual feelings and desires with my partner most of the time.

_____ 2. I find it difficult to talk to my partner about sexual feelings and desires when we are being intimate.

_____ 3. My partner finds it difficult to talk about sexual feelings and desires with me.

_____ 4. My partner finds it difficult to talk to me about sexual feelings and desires when we are being intimate.

_____ 5. I let my partner know how sexually satisfied I am by talking about it when we are not being intimate.

_____ 6. I let my partner know how sexually satisfied I am by talking or making sounds during our intimate moments.

_____ 7. My partner lets me know how sexually satisfied he/she is by talking about it when we are not being intimate.

_____ 8. My partner lets me know how sexually satisfied he/she is by talking or making sounds during our intimate moments.

_____ 9. I feel comfortable telling my partner I want to have sex with him/her.

_____ 10. I feel comfortable telling my partner I want to try something new sexually.

_____ 11. When I feel uncomfortable with something my partner wants to do sexually, I can express those feelings.

_____ 12. My partner and I use a lot of nonverbal communication during sex to let each other know what is pleasing.

_____ 13. I am satisfied with how my partner and I communicate sexually.

Adapted from Wheeless, Lawrence R., Virginia Eman Wheeless, and Raymond Baus. "Sexual Communication, Communication Satisfaction, and Solidarity in the Developmental Stages of Intimate Relationships," *Western Journal of Speech Communication,* 48(3), p. 224, copyright © 1984 by the Western Speech Communication Association. Reprinted by permission of the Western Speech Communication Association.

REFLECTION

The Closer You Get, The Faster I Run

Ira Wolfman writes of something many people share: fear of intimacy. He's a self-admitted "Get close—get away!" guy who has many feelings emerge when faced with intimacy in relationships—for example, nervousness, fear, anger, and craziness. Even though he considers himself to be warm, affectionate, intelligent, and caring, if faced with the possibility that a relationship will become close, he forgets these characteristics when he starts thinking total commitment.

Mr. Wolfman, in speaking with Elaine Hatfield of the University of Hawaii at Manoa, learned that his fears of intimacy matched many of the findings of Professor Hatfield's research and that his fears are shared by many—by women perhaps only slightly less than by men.

What fears do you have about intimacy in relationships? Think about any fears you have about getting close and being intimate. Write down five of them. If you do not have any such fears, write down ones you believe are frequently felt by others you know.

1.

2.

3.

4.

5.

Now, read over the six fears at the end of this article that Mr. Wolfman described. Next, write how you relate to these fears.

According to Hatfield, both men and women need to combine the classically feminine need for connection with the classically masculine need for independence. Presently, therapists use various techniques in teaching couples how to achieve greater intimacy, including (1) encouraging people to accept themselves as they are, to recognize their intimates for what they are . . . and let them be, and to express themselves, and (2) teaching people to deal with their intimate's reactions. But Dr. Hatfield cautions: "As long as men were fleeing from intimacy, women could safely pursue them. Now that men are turning around to face them, women may well find themselves taking flight."

1. Loving means risking hurt, risking loss, risking abandonment.
2. Oh, God! You'll find out who I really am!
3. Making choices means forsaking choices.

4 You're going to use it against me, aren't you?
5. You'll smother me . . . and I'll hate it.
6. You'll smother me . . . and I'll love it.

Source: Ira Wolfman, "The Closer You Get, the Faster I Run." *Ms.*, September 1985, 934–935, 112.

GENDER AND SEXUAL IDENTITY QUESTIONS

Patterns of Communication

Though you have to a degree already revealed how friends, family, and other significant people and events had an impact on your sexual being, you haven't yet been asked to specifically address communication patterns as they relate to the above. You are aware by now that the quality of the communication affects the quality of the relationship.

Take a few minutes to reflect on the quality of your own communication patterns and history by completing the following statements.

- When very young my communication with my parents was . . .

- As I grew older, communication with my parents became . . . because . . .

- As a result of this I felt . . .

- I observed my parents' communication to be . . .

- I believe this affected me . . .

- When it comes to trust, I . . .

- When I think about self-disclosure or revealing myself to another, I . . .

- When close friends disclose facts about themselves to me, my feedback is often . . .

- When conflict occurs with others, I . . .

- My greatest strength as a communicator is my ability to . . .

- My greatest weakness as a communicator is . . .

- As far as communication goes, my greatest desire would be to . . .

- My sexual communication with partners has been . . .

- My feelings about this are . . .

I learned through my parents that sex is not a "dirty" thing. It is the most incredibly wonderful experience that two loving people can share together. It is because of my mom and dad that I believe so strongly in the good that sex can bring to an already close and loving relationship.

—24-year-old Caucasian male

Their regular fights and heated arguments, though never physically abusive, were often cruel and verbally offensive. I remember many times the issue of sex being thrown into the arguments only to be used against or to hurt the other person. Too many nights my mom slept downstairs on the couch. They clearly lacked healthy communication. To me this was not an example of a trusting or loving relationship. While I realize it was their mistakes, it makes me worry about what my relations will become.

—25-year-old Caucasian male looking back at his parents' relationship

CHAPTER 9
SEXUAL EXPRESSION

LEARNING OBJECTIVES

At the conclusion of Chapter 9, students should be able to:

1. Describe the elements of sexual attractiveness along gender and orientation lines and discuss the impact of the halo effect.

2. Discuss sexual attraction, including differences in sexual desire.

3. Explain sexual scripts, including cultural, interpersonal, and intrapersonal scripts with examples of each.

4. Describe the role and function of autoeroticism, including sexual fantasies, dreams, and masturbation, through the life cycle.

5. Identify various types of sensuous touching and their role in sexuality.

6. Describe the various meanings associated with kissing and its role as a form of sexual behavior.

7. Discuss oral-genital sex, including cunnilingus and fellatio, changing attitudes toward it, and varying incidence by ethnicity.

8. Discuss the incidence and types of sexual intercourse.

9. Discuss anal eroticism, varying incidence by sexual orientation and ethnicity, and health concerns.

10. Recognize and define the key terms listed below.

Key Terms

erotophilia	masturbation
erotophobia	pleasuring
autoeroticism	analingus
nocturnal orgasm (or emission)	anal intercourse

PRACTICE TEST QUESTIONS

(For answers see Part IV of this book.)

Multiple Choice

1. Men and women who accept and enjoy their sexuality, seek out sexual situations, and engage in more autoerotic and interpersonal sexual situations are said to be:
    a. erotophobic.
    b. erotophilic.
    c. heteroerotic.
    d. sexual perverts.

2. When sexual scripts enable people to give meaning to their physiological responses, the meaning of which depends on the situation, it is referred to as a/an:
    a. cultural component.
    b. interpersonal component.
    c. intrapersonal component.
    d. anatomical component.

3. Fantasies:
   a. radically alter through adulthood.
   b. serve no function in maintaining our psychic equilibrium.
   c. are a normal aspect of our sexuality.
   d. are dangerous because they are accurate indicators of what sexual activities a person is likely to engage in.

4. Through masturbation, children and adolescents learn:
   a. more about their bodies and what is sexually pleasing.
   b. that there are harmful physical effects associated with this activity.
   c. to simulate sexual intercourse.
   d. nothing about themselves.

5. When do human beings begin masturbatory activity?
   a. during infancy
   b. during childhood
   c. during adolescence
   d. late childhood for boys and adolescence for girls

6. Touching:
   a. is a sign of caring and a signal for arousal.
   b. is usually more significant for new couples than for those who have been together for a longer period of time.
   c. should be directed at the genitals or erogenous zones to be effective.
   d. is straightforward and not subject to interpretation.

7. All of the following statements about fellatio are accurate, EXCEPT
   a. It is the most common form of sexual activity to occur with prostitutes.
   b. Frequency of fellatio is associated with relationship satisfaction among gay men.
   c. Fellatio is now an accepted part of heterosexual lovemaking.
   d. Spitting out and rinsing the mouth after ejaculation provides some protection from HIV.

8. Although criminal statutes against oral sex apply to men and women of all sexual orientations, in recent years sodomy laws have been enforced only against:
   a. minors or those under 21 years of age.
   b. ethnic minorities.
   c. gay men and lesbian women.
   d. they are uniformly enforced

9. Because of HIV, the activity that is potentially the most dangerous is:
   a. cunnilingus or fellatio.
   b. deep kissing.
   c. penile/vaginal intercourse.
   d. anal intercourse.

10. All of the following statements about kissing are accurate, EXCEPT:
   a. Kissing symbolizes intimacy between two individuals.
   b. Kissing is the most acceptable premarital sexual activity.
   c. Kissing is, in general, a safer sex activity.
   d. Kissing does nothave high erotic meaning in most human groups.

True/False

Mark T or F on the line before the statement.

_____ 1. Research has demonstrated that there is one universal standard for what is considered to be sexually attractive.

_____ 2. Fluctuations in sexual desire are a normal part of life.

_____ 3. Masturbation is not a substitute for those who are sexually deprived, but an activity that stimulates and is stimulated by other sexual behavior.

_____ 4. Many people fantasize about things that they would never actually do.

_____ 5. Our gender roles have little or no impact on how we behave sexually.

_____ 6. It is the guilt, rather than the fantasizing itself, that may be harmful to a relationship.

_____ 7. Attitudes toward masturbation and masturbatory behavior do not vary between ethnic groups.

_____ 8. Women who masturbate appear to hold more positive sexual attitudes and are more likely to be orgasmic than women who do not masturbate.

_____ 9. There is virtually nothing a couple can do when they are experiencing problems stemming from differences in sexual desire.

_____ 10. Among gay men, anal intercourse is more common than oral sex.

Fill-In

Choose the correct term from the list at the end of this section.

1. Plans that organize and give direction to our behaviors and that strongly influence our sexual activities as

   men and women are called _____.

2. Sexual activities that involve only the self, including sexual fantasies, masturbation, and erotic dreams, are

   referred to as _____.

3. _____ describes individuals who have generally positive attitudes toward sexuality.

4. The intercourse position that allows a woman to have more control over activity and penetration is the

   _____.

5. Masters and Johnson suggest a form of nongenital touching they call _____.

6. Our earliest interpersonal sexual experience is usually _____.

7. Oral stimulation of a woman's vulva is called _____.

8. Oral stimulation of a man's penis is called _____.

9. A term for the licking of the anal region is _____.

10. Stimulation of the genitals for pleasure is known as _____.

        analingus   kissing
        autoeroticism   masturbation
        cunnilingus   pleasuring
        erotophilia   sexual scripts
        fellatio   woman above

Short Answer

1. Paul and Lisa both want to make passionate love. Describe the likely course of their lovemaking in terms of their sexual scripts.

2. Discuss two functions of sexual fantasy.

3. State three positive functions of masturbation.

4. Describe the forms that nongenital touching and caressing can take and two advantages of this type of pleasuring.

 **OBSERVATION**

Let's Talk About S...E...X

Sex ranks with money and death as being one of the least honestly talked about subjects in our culture. If you are comfortable with the project, interview a trusted friend to assess his or her attitudes and beliefs regarding the behaviors listed below. Request honesty in the interview and provide respect and confidentiality.

What are your:

- preferences regarding sexual attractiveness?

- ways to initiate physical contact in courtship or marriage?

- attitudes about sexual fantasies and dreams?

- thoughts and feelings about masturbation?

- feelings about oral-genital sex?

- thoughts about the importance of touch and caressing?

- preferences regarding sexual intercourse?

- feelings about anal eroticism and intercourse?

What did you learn as a result of this interview and discussion? How do your own thoughts, feelings, and attitudes compare with those of the person you interviewed? What was the most difficult question to ask? Why? What was the easiest questions to ask? Why?

 **REFLECTION**

Rating Sexual Attractiveness

Strong, DeVault, and Sayad review and discuss literature that relates to sexual attractiveness. Acknowledging that different cultures, genders, and individuals view aspects of sexual attractiveness differently and uniquely, take a few minutes to think about what you find attractive in a potential partner. Consider emotional and psychological as well as physical factors. Organize your list in terms of the importance of each feature. Compare your list with what is cited in the textbook. How does it compare? If you wish, share this activity and compare your list with a trusted friend's.

The physical qualities I find most desirable in a potential partner are: **Priority**

_____   _____

_____   _____

_____   _____

_____   _____

_____   _____

_____   _____

The psychological or emotional qualities I find most desirable in a potential partner are: **Priority**

_____   _____

_____   _____

_____   _____

_____   _____

_____   _____

_____   _____

After completing the list, go back and check the emotional and psychological qualities you possess. Do you have the qualities you are looking for?

As a result of doing this what have you learned?

REFLECTION

The Treasure Island Syndrome

Imagine yourself stranded on an island for one week with someone of the opposite sex, or the same sex if you are gay or lesbian. Knowing that your time together would be limited to one week, what characteristics would you desire in this person?

Now imagine that you are on that island for one year. What characteristics would you desire? List these characteristics from the one you desire most to the one that is least important.

How do these lists differ? How important are these characteristics in a long-term dating partner? How can you tell if your partner has these qualities? How far down the list would you go before letting go of the relationship? Which of the above-mentioned qualities do you possess?

If you are in a relationship and are willing to do so, ask your partner to participate in this same activity and then share and compare results.

 **REFLECTION**

Looking at Fantasyland

Nearly everyone has sexual fantasies; however, not everyone takes the time to write them down and, only if they are comfortable, share them with a companion.

Write down two or three of your favorite sexual fantasies. Remember, they are only for you, if you so desire.

Fantasy #1

Fantasy #2

How easy or difficult was it to re-create the sexual scenarios? How did they appear to you once you saw them in writing? Did you become re-aroused or did they lose their impact? If you shared them with a close friend, what was his or her reaction? How comfortable were you while sharing them?

You may choose to do this activity from time to time and observe the changes and common themes that take place over time.

GENDER AND SEXUAL IDENTITY QUESTIONS

Culture and Religion

Because this chapter addresses a number of sexual attitudes and behaviors that have been touched on in earlier gender questions, we choose to highlight only two aspects of gender identity—the cultural and religious ones. These dimensions are particularly relevant to those whose early development followed more traditional lines or whose families placed an emphasis in these areas.

Please respond to the following statements:

Concerning Culture

- The sexual behaviors that my culture approves and emphasizes are . . .

- The sexual behaviors that my culture discourages or prohibits are . . .

- In terms of what my culture has taught me about sexual behavior, I agree with . . .

- In terms of what my culture has taught me about sexual behavior, I disagree with . . .

- I handle the discrepancy between my culture's teachings and my own by . . .
  (Do not complete if you do not feel a discrepancy.)

- In terms of what my culture has taught me about sexual behavior, I plan on passing down to my children . . .

- In traveling, I have been exposed to another culture's view of sexuality and it has affected me by . . .
  (If you have traveled)

Concerning Religion

- The sexual behaviors that my religion approves and emphasizes are . . .

- The sexual behaviors that my religion discourages or prohibits are . . .

- In terms of what my religion has taught me about sexual behavior, I agree with . . .

- In terms of what my religion has taught me about sexual behavior, I disagree with . . .

- I handle the discrepancy between my religion's teachings and my own by . . .
  (Do not complete if you do not feel a discrepancy.)

- In terms of what my religion has taught me about sexual behavior, I plan on passing down to my children . . .

The issue of cultural relationships is the most difficult aspect of my identity. After enrolling in a college speech class, I became more comfortable talking to the opposite sex and with expressing my views, a trait not found in many Nigerian households. My dad didn't approve of my friendships because he believes that the only time a woman should be involved with a man is if it is going to lead to marriage. On the subject of marriage, most Nigerians marry within their own culture. It's at this point in my life where both cultures clashed.
—24-year-old Nigerian American female

I am caught in the middle of two worlds. With this dilemma, I'm not able to find my self-identity, let alone my sexual identity. Am I a Vietnamese trapped within an American culture, or am I really an American trapped within a Vietnamese body? I'm torn apart by what is right in the American culture but might not be right in the Asian culture almost every single day. In her essay, entitled "To Be Or Not To Be," the author concluded that TO BE an American or NOT TO BE an American is one question. TO BE what people want her to be or NOT TO BE herself was the other question.
—22-year-old Vietnamese woman from a family of 11 children

On the wedding night when a man discovered that his new wife was not a virgin, he returned her to her parents. "Poor parents, they were the talk of the town," my mother would tell me.
—20-year-old Latina describes her mother's story that has scared her for years

Religion was always an important part of my family life, but it appears that it did not have that great of an impact on my early sexual identity. However, as I have gotten older and more specifically in the last few years, religion has once again come into my life and now plays a significant role in my attitudes toward sex. I try to follow the teachings, but this is extremely difficult for me now because I love sex so much. There always seems to be a constant battle going on inside my head of what is acceptable as compared to that which is not.
—22-year-old Caucasian

CHAPTER 10
ATYPICAL AND PARAPHILIC SEXUAL BEHAVIOR

LEARNING OBJECTIVES

At the conclusion of Chapter 10, students should be able to:

1. Compare and contrast atypical and paraphilic sexual behavior.

2. Discuss cross-dressing in popular and gay culture and as a form of "gender relaxation."

3. Discuss domination and submission as atypical behavior, including bondage, the domination and submission subculture, and body piercing and tattooing.

4. Describe briefly the characteristics of paraphiliacs.

5. Describe and characterize the noncoercive paraphilias, including fetishism, and transvestism.

6. Describe and characterize the coercive paraphilias, including zoophilia, voyeurism, exhibitionism, telephone scatologia and frotteurism, and necrophilia.

7. Describe pedophilia, including types of pedophiles, cross-sex and same-sex pedophilia, and female pedophilia.

8. Discuss sexual sadism and sexual masochism, including autoerotic asphyxia.

9. Recognize and define the key terms listed below.

Key Terms

atypical sexual behavior
paraphilia
nymphomania
satyriasis
domination and submission (D/S)
sadomasochism (S&M)
bondage and discipline (B&D)
dominatrix
paraphiliacs
fetishism
transvestism
fetishistic transvestism

zoophilia
voyeurism
exhibitionism
telephone scatologia
frotteurism
necrophilia
pedophilia
pedophile
sexual sadism
sexual masochism
cross-dressing
autoerotic asphyxia

PRACTICE TEST QUESTIONS

(For answers see Part IV of this book.)

Multiple Choice

1. Sexual behaviors that are indicative of mental disorders are called:
   a. atypical sexual behaviors.
   b. abnormal sexual behaviors.
   c. paraphilias.
   d. none of the above

2. Frank and Laura occasionally like to get together with other married couples and engage in group sexual activities (using safer sex techniques, of course). Bill finds this repugnant and states that Frank and Laura are paraphiliacs and are mentally disturbed. This demonstrates how
   a. clinical terms can be used judgmentally and moralistically.
   b. untrained individuals can accurately diagnose paraphilias.
   c. there are many undetected paraphiliacs in society.
   d. prevalent satyriasis is among married couples.

3. The critical element in domination and submission is:
   a. pain.
   b. power.
   c. whips.
   d. intimacy.

4. Which of these is NOT a form of domination and submission?
   a. bondage and discipline
   b. humiliation
   c. kennelism
   d. stabbing

5. According to the authors, each of the following is a characteristic of paraphiliacs EXCEPT:
   a. they are most likely to be males ranging in age from 45–65.
   b. they have a strong need to act out long-standing, unusual erotic sexual fantasies.
   c. they are unable to have a conventional sexual relationship.
   d. they are most likely to be males ranging in age from 15–25.

6. All of the following are considered noncoercive paraphilias EXCEPT:
   a. fetishism.
   b. exhibitionism.
   c. transvestism.
   d. domination and submission.

7. What is the recommended clinical treatment for transvestites?
   a. Use aversion therapy.
   b. Use drug therapy.
   c. Use intense psychotherapy.
   d. Help the transvestite and those close to him accept his cross-dressing.

8. What profession is likely for a necrophiliac?
   a. criminal
   b. medical doctor
   c. mortician
   d. soldier

9. The difference between coercive paraphilias and noncoercive paraphilias is:
   a. the age of the youngest participant.
   b. coercive paraphilias involve victimization and cause harm.
   c. coercive paraphilias involve more than one other person.
   d. men participate in coercive paraphilias whereas women enjoy noncoercive paraphilias.

10. Which paraphilia is responsible for the most arrests?
    a. voyeurism
    b. transvestism
    c. exhibitionism
    d. frotteurism

11. Sexual contact between adult females and young boys (12 or younger):
    a. only rarely occurs.
    b. has never been reported.
    c. is more common than most people realize.
    d. is always regarded as negative by the boy.

12. The most frequent sexual activity in cross-sex pedophilia is
    a. oral stimulation.
    b. touching and fondling of genitals.
    c. intercourse.
    d. anal stimulation.

True/False

Mark T or F on the line before the statement.

_____ 1. The terms *atypical sexual behaviors* and *abnormal sexual behaviors* describe the same thing.

_____ 2. Atypical sexual behavior refers to any non-reproductive sexual activity.

_____ 3. Paraphilias are much more likely to occur among gay men and bisexuals than among heterosexuals.

_____ 4. The main focus in frotteurism is making obscene verbal statements.

_____ 5. A majority of women have been victimized by a coercive paraphiliac.

_____ 6. Exhibitionists usually only expose themselves to strangers or near strangers.

_____ 7. If a heterosexually-identified man is a pedophile he molests only girls.

_____ 8. Almost all transvestites are homosexuals.

_____ 9. Probably the best way to respond to an obscene telephone caller is to act shocked and angry.

_____ 10. Sexual addiction is believed by most psychologists and researchers to be a paraphilia and is recognized as a dysfunction by the American Psychological Association.

Fill-In

Choose the correct term from the list at the end of this section.

1. The negative term commonly used to describe abnormal or excessive sexual desire in a woman is

   _____.

2. The term _____ is used to refer to sexual arousal derived from the consensual acting out of sexual scenes in which one person dominates and the other submits.

3. A woman specializing in "discipline" in sexual scenes is known as a _____.

4. The sexualization of and fixation on inanimate objects is known as _____.

5. Sexual excitement derived from animals is known as bestiality or _____.

6. The name of the paraphilia where there is sexual rubbing against another person without their consent is

   _____.

7. Sexual excitement from secretly watching another person who is nude, disrobing, or engaging in sexual

   activity is known as _____.

8. The intense recurring urge to display one's genitals to an unsuspecting stranger is known as

   _____.

9. Recurrent intense sexual urges and sexually arousing fantasies involving sexual activity with children is

   called _____.

10. A life-threatening paraphilia that involves self-strangulation during masturbation is called

   _____.

autoerotic asphyxia	frotteurism
domination and submission	nymphomania
dominatrix	pedophilia
exhibitionism	voyeurism
fetishism	zoophilia

Short Answer

1. Compare and contrast coercive and noncoercive sexual behavior and give examples of each.

2. What advice does the textbook give about how to deal with obscene phone calls?

3. What are the similarities and differences between cross-sex pedophilia and same-sex pedophilia?

 **OBSERVATION**

Does It Happen in My Community?

This activity gives you a chance to find out about paraphilic sexual behavior in the area where you live. Contact your police department and ask to talk to the person in charge of sex-related crimes. Ask which of the behaviors discussed in the chapter have been reported to authorities within the last year.

Have any reports led to arrests?

Have they seen an increase in any type of sex-related crime?

When people are arrested as exhibitionists or voyeurs, are they usually handled by court action leading to jail or by psychological counseling or both?

What is the attitude of the person you talked to toward people who have paraphilias?

 **OBSERVATION**

The Media and Atypical Sexual Behavior

How are atypical or paraphilic behaviors treated by the media? When they do appear on television, is it usually on crime or talk shows? If you have seen any shows dealing with behaviors discussed in this chapter, answer these questions.

What atypical behavior was shown?

What role did it have in the plot of the program?

What attitude was conveyed about this behavior?

How did you feel about the way the behavior was handled?

Cross-dressing has been a common theme in movies. Watch one of the movies that explore this issue, such as *Some Like It Hot, Tootsie, Torch Song Trilogy, Crying Game, Priscilla, Queen of the Desert,* or *Mrs. Doubtfire* and answer these questions.

What were the motives for the cross-dressing?

What role did it have in the plot of the movie?

How did others respond to this behavior?

How did you feel about the way cross-dressing was handled in the film?

REFLECTION

Sexual Attitudes and Legal Sanctions

This activity gives you the opportunity to examine your feelings and attitudes toward the variety of sexual activities discussed in this chapter and the legal sanctions, if any, that you feel should be applied to each of these activities.

Check the column that best matches the way you feel about each behavior.

Use this key to help you mark the chart:

Attitudes:

A. normal and acceptable
B. acceptable
C. abnormal
D. major psychological disturbance

Legal Sanctions:

A. repeal all laws regulating this activity
B. decriminalize, require treatment
C. misdemeanor, short-term sentence (one year or less)
D. felony, long-term sentence
E. mandatory counseling (and possible prison term)

	ATTITUDES				LEGAL SANCTIONS				
Sexual Activity	**A**	**B**	**C**	**D**	**A**	**B**	**C**	**D**	**E**
domination and submission									
bondage and discipline									
babyism									
kennelism									
fetishism									
fetishistic transvestism									
zoophilia									
voyeurism									
exhibitionism									
telephone scatalogia									
frotteurism									
necrophilia									
pedophilia									
sexual sadism and sexual masochism									

 **OBSERVATION**

Body Play: What's It All About

We see (and perhaps know) people who have strategically placed tattoos or piercings and may wonder what prompted them to do it in the first place and what reactions they have now that it is done. For the sake of research, now is the time to ask.

Find someone who has either a tattoo or piercing (other than the earlobe) and, reserving judgment, inquire about the following:

- What kind of pierce or tattoo do you have? When was it done?

- By whom did you receive the procedure(s)? Was it painful?

- How was it performed?

- Would you say the conditions were sterile? Was that something that concerned you?

- Did you have any problems with the procedure or follow-up?

- Why did you choose the site (if pierced) or illustration (if tattooed)?

- Does it meet your expectations?

- What are your feelings now that you've had it done?

- Do you plan to have additional piercing or tatooing? If you no longer desire to have it how would you have it removed?

GENDER AND SEXUAL IDENTITY QUESTIONS

Atypical and Paraphilic Sexual Behavior

- Sometimes I wonder if I am normal because . . .

- I find the idea of getting a tattoo and/or the idea of body piercing . . .

- I find the idea of participating in exhibitionist behavior . . .

- I find the idea of participating in voyeuristic behavior . . .

- The sexual activity I find myself most attracted to is . . .

- The sexual activity I find most repugnant is . . .

- I have encountered a _____ and it made me feel . . .
  (paraphiliac such as exhibitionist, obscene phone caller)

- I have engaged in sexual practices that may be physically or psychologically harmful to myself or others when . . .

- I have/have not gotten into therapy about this because . . .

- If someone in my family (parent, sister, brother, uncle) was involved in a paraphilic behavior I would feel . . .

I'd been smoking pot regularly since 14 and drinking since about 16. After my fling with the older woman, I began to use more heavily and experimented with hallucinogens and amphetamines. It was just a general trend to try new things that I wasn't supposed to. I was a risk taker. Peer pressure to use drugs and achieve sexual experiences were closely related. I later moved to Berkeley to attend school, but the only education I got was through drugs and sex.

—27-year-old Caucasian male

I am no stranger to sexual paraphilias but seeing a man's erect penis pointed in my face while I busily searched for a library book deeply upset me. The exhibitionist chose a most public forum—the local library which was literally attached to the police department. Upon seeing him and observing children studying merely one aisle away, I scrambled to the front desk and asked that the police be called. Hearing my request, the man chose to remain in place and was quickly apprehended. The element of surprise caught me off guard, but the element of guilt appeared to motivate him to choose and remain in a place where his violation could be recognized and punished. I still wonder, sometimes, why this incident upset me so.

—44-year-old Caucasian female

CHAPTER 11
CONTRACEPTION AND BIRTH CONTROL

LEARNING OBJECTIVES

At the conclusion of Chapter 11, students should be able to:

1. Explain the psychology of contraceptive risk taking and discuss the issues involved in choosing a reliable method.

2. List and describe hormonal methods of contraception (including oral contraceptives, implants, and injections) and their effectiveness, advantages, and possible problems.

3. List and describe barrier methods of contraception (including condoms, diaphragm, cervical cap, and female condoms) and their effectiveness, advantages, and possible problems.

4. Describe spermicides (including contraceptive foam, film, creams, and jellies) and their effectiveness, advantages, and possible problems.

5. Describe the IUD (intrauterine device) and its effectiveness, advantages, and possible problems.

6. List and describe fertility awareness methods (including calendar, BBT, mucus method, and sympto-thermal) and their effectiveness, advantages, and possible problems.

7. List and describe sterilization methods and their effectiveness, advantages, and possible problems.

8. Discuss emergency contraception methods (including morning-after pill, mini-pill, and copper IUD) and their effectiveness, advantages, and possible problems.

9. Discuss abortion, including methods, prevalence, characteristics of women having abortions and their reasons, and men and abortion; and delineate the arguments in the abortion debate.

10. Discuss reasons that research into new contraceptive methods has been limited.

11. Recognize and define the key terms listed below.

Key Terms

birth control
conceptus
contraception
abstinence
outercourse
oral contraceptive
implant
Norplant
Depo-Provera (DMPA)
coitus interruptus
male condom
female condom
diaphragm
cervical cap

spermicide
nonoxynol-9
bioadhesive gel
contraceptive foam
contraceptive film
intrauterine device (IUD)
fertility awareness method
calendar (rhythm) method
basal body temperature (BBT)
cervical mucus method
symptothermal method
sterilization or voluntary
    surgical contraception
tubal ligation

laparoscopy
minilaparotomy
vasectomy
emergency contraception (also called
    postcoital birth control)
menstrual extraction
mifepristone with misoprostol
    (formerly known as RU-486)
abortion
spontaneous abortion
laminaria
vacuum aspiration
dilation and curettage (D & C)
dilation and evacuation (D & E)
hysterotomy

PRACTICE TEST QUESTIONS

(For answers see Part IV of this book.)

Multiple Choice

1. All of the following factors increase the likelihood that a couple will use contraception, EXCEPT:
   a. planning the first intercourse.
   b. increasing age of the sexually active person.
   c. explicit discussion of contraception.
   d. being in a casual dating relationship.

2. When comparing different contraceptive techniques, Myra examines figures on "user effectiveness." This refers to:
   a. how effective the method is if used in laboratory conditions (i.e., perfectly and consistently).
   b. the level of disease protection the method offers.
   c. the level of effectiveness when in actual use.
   d. the aesthetic factors involved in using the method.

3. The intrauterine device or IUD:
   a. has been permanently withdrawn from the U.S. market.
   b. is inserted into the fallopian tubes and remains there until expelled or withdrawn.
   c. can remain in place from one year to indefinitely, depending on the type of device.
   d. has clearly identified ways of preventing pregnancy.

4. Which is the most common form of contraception among married couples in the United States?
   a. the pill
   b. the diaphragm
   c. sterilization
   d. the IUD

5. According to the text, what makes a contraceptive technique the *best* method for a person?
   a. the cost, both immediate and long-term
   b. aesthetics
   c. popular opinion regarding frequency of use
   d. likelihood of consistent use

6. How does a diaphragm work?
   a. It pushes sperm outside of the vagina.
   b. It kills sperm in the vagina.
   c. It prevents sperm from entering the cervix.
   d. It prevents eggs from entering the uterus.

7. The chief reason for latex condom failures is:
   a. user mishandling.
   b. manufacturing defects.
   c. insufficient size.
   d. allergic reactions.

8. Which is NOT a common side effect when a women starts taking birth control pills?
   a. breast tenderness
   b. nausea or vomiting
   c. weight gain or loss
   d. smaller breast size

9. Condoms can be used with
   a. oil-based lubricants.
   b. Vaseline.
   c. water-based lubricants.
   d. no lubricants, because any kind of lubricant weakens condoms and makes them more likely to tear.

10. The health risks of taking the birth control pill are increased if the woman:
    a. is overweight.
    b. smokes.
    c. has low blood pressure.
    d. has heavy periods.

11. The contraceptive implant containing progestin, which is slowly released over a period of up to 5 years, is called:
    a. RU-486.
    b. Depo-Provera.
    c. Norplant.
    d. nonoxynol-9.

12. Which is NOT one of the fertility awareness methods?
    a. calendar (rhythm) method
    b. culpotomy method
    c. basal body temperature method
    d. mucus (Billings) method

13. The most common form of sterilization for women in this country is:
    a. tubal ligation.
    b. culpotomy.
    c. culdoscopy.
    d. hysterectomy.

14. John had a vasectomy three weeks ago. This means that he:
    a. can have unprotected intercourse and not worry about a pregnancy because he is no longer fertile.
    b. could still be fertile and needs to wait a few weeks before depending on his vasectomy for contraception.
    c. will have a more watery ejaculate than he had before.
    d. will not have any ejaculate when he has an orgasm.

15. The earliest form of abortion now available is the:
    a. vacuum aspiration.
    b. dilation and curettage (D & C).
    c. dilation and evacuation (D & E).
    d. suction method.

Fill-In

Choose the correct term from the list at the end of the section.

1. _____ is any means of preventing a birth from taking place, while _____ is the prevention of conception altogether.

2. The term used to describe refraining from sexual intercourse is _____, but it does not mean people can't have other sexual activity that provides sexual satisfaction.

3. A contraceptive device that also guards against the transmission of certain disease organisms is the

   _____.

4. The calendar, basal body temperature, and Billings methods are all examples of _____.

5. A _____ is a rubber cup with a flexible rim that is placed inside the vagina blocking the cervix, while a _____ is a small rubber barrier device that fits snugly over the cervix and is held in place by suction.

6. To gradually expand the cervical opening, a health-care practitioner may insert a _____ several hours before an abortion.

7. The surgical method of abortion that is performed under local anesthesia in the first trimester and uses dilation followed by suction is called _____.

8. Tubal ligation and vasectomy are examples of _____.

9. Second trimester methods of abortion include _____, where the cervix is dilated and the fetus removed by alternating solution and curettage.

10. Surgical removal of the uterus is called _____.

abstinence	hysterectomy
birth control	laminaria
cervical cap	latex or polyurethane condom
contraception	Norplant
diaphragm	spontaneous abortion
dilation and curettage (D & C)	sterilization
dilation and evacuation (D & E)	vacuum aspiration
fertility awareness	

Matching

1. birth control _____
2. contraception _____
3. Norplant _____
4. Depo-Provera (DMPA) _____
5. nonoxynol-9 _____
6. RU-486 _____
7. diaphragm _____
8. spontaneous abortion _____

a. The injectable contraceptive that lasts from 3 to 6 months.

b. The most widely used spermicide in the United States.

c. The prevention of conception altogether.

d. Must be used with a spermicidal cream or gel in order to be effective.

e. Means of preventing birth from taking place.

f. Contraceptive implant that contains progestin, is implanted under a woman's skin, and lasts for 5 years.

g. Commonly referred to as "miscarriage."

h. A postcoital method of birth control that involves taking a pill to induce endometrial shedding.

Short Answer

1. What are some ways that men can take contraceptive responsibility?

2. List and discuss the benefits and drawbacks of taking birth control pills.

3. Women are buying between 40% and 90% of the condoms sold. What are the four key points concerning women and condom use?

4. Compare and contrast the pro-life and pro-choice arguments.

OBSERVATION

Facts About Contraception

To help you choose the best method of contraception for you and your partner, you must first be familiar with the advantages, disadvantages, and effectiveness ratings of the different methods. Fill in the boxes below with the appropriate comments, using your text if necessary.

Method	Advantages	Disadvantages	Effectiveness
Oral contraceptives			
Norplant implants			
DMPA (Depo-Provera injections)			
IUDs • Copper T-380A • Progestasert			
Male Condom			
Female Condom			

(continued on next page)

Method	Advantages	Disadvantages	Effectiveness
Diaphragm with spermicide			
Cervical cap			
Vaginal spermicides			
Fertility awareness method			
Withdrawal			
Male sterilization			
Female sterilization			

REFLECTION

Your Reproductive Life Plan

Birth control must fit into your reproductive life plan. Ask yourself these questions to help you work out your personal reproductive life plan.

- Would I like to have children one day? Why or why not?

- Would I like to be married/partnered one day?

- Would I like to wait until I'm married to start having sexual intercourse?

- At what point during or after my education would I like to be married?

- How old would I like to be when I have my first child?

- How many children would I like to have? How many years apart would they be spaced?

- How would I feel if I were not able to have any children?

- If I (or my partner) had an unplanned pregnancy, would I consider having, or encourage my partner to have, an abortion?

- Would I like to work when my children are young? If so, at what point in their development would I return to work? How much would I work?

- Of all the things I could do in my life, what is the most important for me to accomplish?

- How would children affect this goal?

- What would it mean to me if my marriage were to end in divorce?

- How does my life plan fit in with my ethical or religious beliefs?

- How do my current health and health habits affect my ability to conceive and to be a parent?

REFLECTION

Birth Control Continuum

1. Now that you are knowledgeable about the various methods of birth control, indicate how you feel about these methods by placing the number for each one at the appropriate point on the following continuum. Try to enter each one.

    1. abortion
    2. abstinence
    3. male condom
    4. Depo-Provera (DMPA)
    5. diaphragm with spermicide

    6. foam
    7. female condom
    8. spermicide with condom
    9. IUD
    10. morning-after pill

    11. Norplant
    12. nothing
    13. pill
    14. rhythm

    15. RU-486
    16. tubal ligation
    17. vasectomy
    18. withdrawal

    Very   **No**   **Very**
    Unacceptable   **Feeling**   **Acceptable**

    |—————————————————————————|—————————————————————————|

2. Using the same list as in number 1, indicate how you feel about others using these methods.

    Very   **No**   **Very**
    Unacceptable   **Feeling**   **Acceptable**

    |—————————————————————————|—————————————————————————|

3. Discuss how you feel about using the method you think is most appropriate for yourself and/or your partner. Take into consideration the "hassle factor," how you feel about touching your body, and the cost, safety, and convenience aspects of the method. If appropriate, you may choose to share and discuss this exercise with your partner.

REFLECTION

Taking Sexual Risks

1. After reading the discussion in the text of Kristen Luker's study on risk taking, do you think this applies to you?

    Do you take sexual risks? What kind? Why?

    Do you take risks in other areas of your life? For example, if you were late to an appointment but needed to get gas, would you go on and hope there was enough gas, waiting until on the way home to stop at the gas station?

    Do the two (risk taking in general and risk taking during sex) overlap?

2. After doing the exercises in this chapter about feelings and attitudes toward birth control, what have you learned? Knowing your attitudes toward birth control and risk taking, do you think you are likely to take chances?

 **OBSERVATION**

Thinking About Abortion

To help define your own position on abortion, answer the following series of questions.

	Agree	Disagree
1. The fertilized egg is a human being from the moment of conception.	_____	_____
2. The rights of the fetus at any stage take precedence over any decision a woman might want to make regarding her pregnancy.	_____	_____
3. The rights of the fetus depend upon its gestational age: Further along in the pregnancy, the fetus has more rights.	_____	_____
4. Each individual woman should have final say over decisions regarding her health and body; politicians should not be allowed to decide.	_____	_____
5. In cases of teenagers seeking an abortion, parental consent should be required.	_____	_____
6. In cases of married women seeking an abortion, spousal consent should be required.	_____	_____
7. In cases of late abortion, tests should be done to determine the viability of the fetus.	_____	_____
8. The federal government should provide public funding for abortion to ensure equal access to abortion for all women.	_____	_____
9. The federal government should not allow states to pass their own abortion laws; there should be uniform laws for the entire country.	_____	_____

10. Does a woman's right to choose whether or not to have an abortion depend upon the circumstances surrounding conception or the situation of the mother? In which of the following situations, if any, would you support a woman's right to choose to have an abortion (check where appropriate)?

_____ An abortion is necessary to maintain the woman's life or health.

_____ The pregnancy is a result of rape or incest.

_____ A serious birth defect has been detected in the fetus through amniocentesis or chorionic villus sampling.

_____ The pregnancy is a result of the failure of a contraceptive method or device.

_____ The pregnancy occurred when no contraceptive method was in use.

_____ A single mother, pregnant for the fifth time, wants an abortion because she feels she cannot support another child.

_____ A pregnant 15-year-old high school student feels having a child would prove to be too great a disruption in her life and keep her from reaching her goals for the future.

_____ A pregnant 19-year-old college student does not want to interrupt her education.

_____ The father of the child has stated he will provide no support and is not interested in helping raise the child.

_____ Parents of two boys wish to terminate the mother's pregnancy because the fetus is male rather than female.

On the basis of your answers, describe your position on abortion. Should it be legal or illegal? Are there certain circumstances in which it should or should not be allowed? What sorts of rules should govern when it can be performed?

GENDER AND SEXUAL IDENTITY QUESTIONS

Use of Birth Control

After reading the textbook, we hope you have gained some additional understanding about how attitudes, feelings, and beliefs about birth control and risk taking affect behavior. Review the questions below and, if you are or have been sexually active, respond to them as honestly as you can.

- The first time I had sex I did/didn't use birth control because . . .

- I usually talk to someone about birth control before/after we have intercourse because . . .

- Talking about birth control with a partner makes me feel . . .

- My feelings when I went to get birth control from the doctor or clinic were . . .

- When I bought birth control supplies, I felt . . .

- I (and/or my partner) have been faced with a decision about abortion and that was . . .

- When someone close to me had to deal with abortion, I felt . . .

- My feelings about abortion now are . . .

I didn't know much about abortion, but I knew that it was a way out and I was going to try anything. I ended up going to my best friend's house to look through her yellow pages in order to find cheap clinics. By doing this, I ended up in one of the worst abortion clinics you could imagine. I remember that there was only one nurse who was also the receptionist and about two doctors at the most. As I lay on the examination table, I remember seeing ants crawling around the place, and it looked like a meat market. As I walked into the actual abortion room, I could see something that held the aborted babies. All I can say at this point of my life is that I am glad to be alive.
—22-year-old African American female

We began to have sex but tried not to have intercourse. We made promises to each other that one person would always keep an article of clothing on to act as a barrier in case our passion got out of control. Well, needless to say, that plan never worked very well. To this day I ask myself why we did not get some type of birth control, especially when we realized our relationship was going to last for a while. It does not take much to figure out the answer to that question. I felt guilty about being in a sexual relationship, and actively pursuing birth control would have meant I knew what I was doing and was choosing to go against what I had been taught was wrong.
—33-year-old Caucasian female recalling her first sexual experience

CHAPTER 12
CONCEPTION, PREGNANCY, AND CHILDBIRTH

LEARNING OBJECTIVES

At the conclusion of Chapter 12, students should be able to:

1. Describe the fertilization process and development of the conceptus.

2. Discuss the pregnant woman's relationship to her partner and sexuality during pregnancy.

3. List and describe the possible complications of pregnancy, including teratogens, diseases, conditions, low birth weight, and fetal diagnosis.

4. Discuss pregnancy loss, including spontaneous abortion, infant mortality rates, and coping with loss.

5. List the principal causes of male and female infertility, and discuss emotional responses to infertility, treatments, surrogate motherhood, and ethical issues.

6. Describe the stages of labor and delivery.

7. Discuss childbirth choices, including hospital births, C-sections, prepared childbirth, birthing rooms and centers, and home births.

8. Discuss the question of circumcision, including religious, cultural, and health considerations.

9. Discuss breast-feeding, including the physiology, benefits, and issues involved in choosing to breast-feed.

10. Discuss becoming a parent, including the postpartum period, parental roles, gay/lesbian parenting, and coping with stress.

11. Recognize and define the key terms listed below.

Key Terms

child-free
diploid zygote
blastocyst
implantation
embryo
fetus
gestation
embryonic membranes
amnio
amniotic fluid
lanugo
placenta
umbilical cord
agglutination test
Hegar's sign
teratogens
ectopic pregnancy
   (also known as tubal pregnancy)
toxemia

preeclampsia
low birth weight (LBW)
ultrasonography
   (also known as ultrasound)
sonogram
amniocentesis
chorionic villus sampling (CVS)
alpha-feto protein (AFP) screening
spontaneous abortion
sudden infant death syndrome (SIDS)
infertility
pelvic inflammatory disease (PID)
endometriosis
varicocele
intrauterine insemination (IUI)
artificial insemination (AI)
therapeutic donor insemination (TDI)
in vitro fertilization (IVF)
gamete intrafallopian transfer (GIFT)
zygote intrafallopian transfer (ZIFT)

surrogate motherhood
parturition
Braxton Hicks contractions
effacement
dilation
oxytocin
transition
vernix
neonate
Apgar score
involution
lochia
episiotomy
cesarean section, or C-section
prepared childbirth
circumcision
lactation
colostrum
postpartum period

PRACTICE TEST QUESTIONS

(For answers see Part IV of this book.)

Multiple Choice

1. The current use of the term "childfree" to replace the term "childless" reflects:
   a. that couples who don't have children today are viewed as lacking fulfillment.
   b. the shift of values in our culture that sees not having children as a choice with positive advantages.
   c. that women who choose to be childfree are usually poorly educated.
   d. none of the above

2. Studies of childfree marriages indicate:
   a. a higher degree of marital adjustment or satisfaction than is found among couples with children.
   b. a lower degree of marital adjustment or satisfaction than is found among couples with children.
   c. that divorce is more probable in childfree marriages.
   d. both a and c

3. To increase the likelihood of fertilization, intercourse should occur:
   a. ten days after the first day of the menstrual cycle.
   b. from three days before through one day after ovulation.
   c. from one to five days before menstruation begins.
   d. in the three days before and two days after the menstrual period.

4. The nutrients from Lucille's delicious dinner are passed to her developing fetus via the
   a. amniotic fluid.
   b. chorion.
   c. yolk sac.
   d. placenta.

5. Pregnancy tests detect the presence of what hormone secreted by the implanted blastocyst?
   a. estrogen
   b. testosterone
   c. HCG (human chorionic gonadotropin)
   d. amnion

6. The trimester of pregnancy during which the expectant mother is most likely to experience nausea, fatigue, and swelling of the breasts is usually the:
   a. first trimester.
   b. second trimester.
   c. third trimester.
   d. second trimester if she is having a boy.

7. Which of the following statements concerning sexual activity and pregnancy is correct?
   a. Most doctors advise no sexual activity for women after the third month of pregnancy.
   b. Orgasms are considered harmful to most pregnant women after the fifth month of pregnancy.
   c. Unless a woman has a medical problem, sexual activity should present no problems during pregnancy.
   d. Most couples have no desire for sexual activity during pregnancy.

8. At the present time, most experts counsel pregnant women to:
   a. drink no more than one beer or one glass of wine per day.
   b. drink beer, wine, or other alcohol only after the fourth month, since vital organs are already formed.
   c. abstain entirely from alcohol because there is no safe dosage known at this time.
   d. drink whatever they normally do but stay away from street drugs.

9. Cigarette smoking in pregnant women:
   a. has not been shown to affect babies if their mothers smoke less than a pack a day.
   b. produces babies who weigh less at birth than babies born to nonsmokers.
   c. has been implicated in sudden infant death syndrome, respiratory disorders in children, and various adverse pregnancy outcomes.
   d. both b and c.

10. Tina is 42 years old and pregnant. Because of a higher likelihood of Down Syndrome, her health care practitioner is likely to recommend:
    a. alpha-feto protein (AFP).
    b. HCG testing.
    c. amniocentesis or chorionic villus sampling (CVS).
    d. ultrasound.

11. Most miscarriages are due to:
    a. chromosomal abnormalities.
    b. too much exercise.
    c. intercourse during pregnancy.
    d. poor nutrition.

12. Circumcision:
    a. has been routinely performed on newborn boys in the United States since the 1930s.
    b. is often done without anesthesia.
    c. has no medical indication for or against it.
    d. all of the above are true

13. The most common cause of female infertility is:
    a. environmental toxicity.
    b. a history of previous abortion.
    c. fallopian tube blockage due to PID.
    d. lack of ovulation.

14. The longest stage of labor is:
    a. the first stage.
    b. the second stage.
    c. the third stage.
    d. none, they are all equal in time

15. All of the following are true about the postpartum period EXCEPT:
    a. all women say this is one of the happiest times of their lives.
    b. it may create considerable stress.
    c. fathers are also affected and feel stress.
    d. biological, psychological, and social factors can all affect the postpartum period.

Fill-In

Choose the correct term from the list at the end of the section.

1. Substances that cause defects in developing embryos or fetuses are known as _____.

2. In an _____ pregnancy, the fertilized egg can implant itself in the fallopian tube.

3. The fertility treatment where sperm and oocyte are combined in a laboratory dish and later the pre-embryo is

    implanted is called _____.

4. The fertility treatment where sperm and eggs are collected and deposited together in the fallopian tube is

    known as _____.

5. The fertility treatment where semen is deposited by syringe near the opening of the cervix is known as

    _____.

6. The test where fluid from the uterus is tested for birth defects is called _____.

7. The process of one woman having a baby for another woman is known as _____.

8. During labor, the thinning of the cervix is known as _____.

9. During labor, the widening of the opening of the cervix is known as _____.

10. During delivery, the mother will probably be given a(an) _____, a surgical procedure that
    enlarges the vaginal opening by cutting through the perineum toward the anus.

amniocentesis	episiotomy
artificial insemination	gamete intrafallopian transfer
dilation	in vitro fertilization
ectopic	surrogate motherhood
effacement	teratogens

Matching 1

1. blastocyst _____

2. embryo _____

3. fetus _____

4. umbilical cord _____

5. lanugo _____

6. chorion _____

7. placenta _____

a. The term for the conceptus for the first 8 weeks.

b. The name given a zygote after 4 or 5 days, containing about 100 cells.

c. The term for the human offspring or conceptus after the eighth week.

d. The organ formed in early pregnancy through which the fetus receives oxygen and nutrients and gets rid of waste.

e. The fine, downy hair that covers the fetus.

f. The embryo's outermost membrane.

g. The structure that attaches the mother's bloodstream to the fetus.

Matching 2

1. ultrasound _____

2. sonogram _____

3. amniocentesis _____

4. chorionic villus sampling _____ (CVS)

5. alpha-feto protein (AFP) screening _____

a. Procedure, either through the abdomen or cervix involving removal of tiny pieces of membrane that encase the embryo to test for chromosomal abnormalities.

b. Procedure where amniotic fluid is withdrawn from the uterus through the abdominal wall of the mother and is tested for chromosomal abnormalities.

c. Uses high-frequency sound waves to create a picture of the fetus in the uterus.

d. Test performed between the 9th and 11th week of pregnancy to reveal chromosomal abnormalities.

e. The picture made by ultrasound of the fetus in the uterus.

Matching 3

1. artificial insemination (AI) _____

2. therapeutic donor insemination (TDI) _____

3. in vitro fertilization (IVF) _____

4. gamete intrafallopian transfer (GIFT) _____

5. zygote intrafallopian transfer (ZIFT) _____

a. Egg and sperm are united in a petri dish and then transferred immediately to the fallopian tubes.

b. Sperm and eggs are collected from parents and deposited together in the fallopian tubes.

c. Partner's semen is deposited by syringe near the cervical opening.

d. Sperm from a donor is deposited by syringe near the cervical opening.

e. Combining sperm and oocyte in a laboratory dish and then implanting the blastocyst into the uterus.

Short Answer

1. List the variety of feelings that women and their partners may experience during pregnancy. What types of changes can occur in their relationship as a result of the pregnancy?

   Woman:

   Partner:

   Relationship changes:

2. What recommendations and suggestions do doctors usually make concerning sexual behavior during pregnancy?

3. What feelings can pregnant women experience as the result of a loss of pregnancy and/or child before or during birth? What steps can help in the healing process?

4. Describe the emotional responses couples can have to infertility and what treatment options are available.

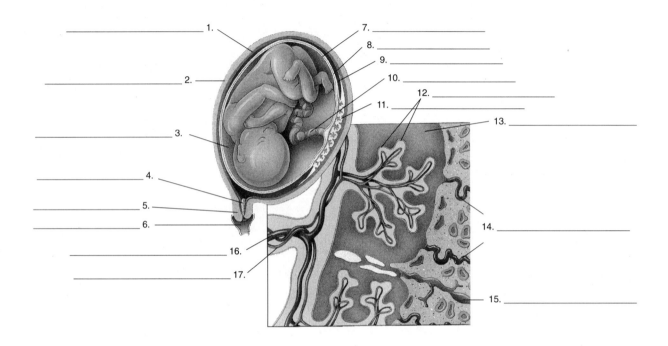

1. _____
2. _____
3. _____
4. _____
5. _____
6. _____
16. _____
17. _____

7. _____
8. _____
9. _____
10. _____
12. _____
11. _____
13. _____
14. _____
15. _____

Label the Diagram

a. amnion
b. amniotic cavity filled with amniotic fluid
c. cervix
d. chorion
e. chorionic villi
f. lining of uterus (endometrium)
g. maternal blood collects
h. maternal endometrial arterioles
i. maternal endometrial venule

j. mucous plug
k. muscle layer of uterine wall
l. placenta
m. umbilical arteries
n. umbilical cord
o. umbilical vein
p. uterine cavity
q. vagina (birth canal)

1. ____   9. ____
2. ____   10. ____
3. ____   11. ____
4. ____   12. ____
5. ____   13. ____
6. ____   14. ____
7. ____   15. ____
8. ____   16. ____
          17. ____

 **OBSERVATION**

The Childbirth Experience

Interview two or three friends who have experienced childbirth and discuss with them their experiences, perceptions, and feelings about the approach they chose to deliver their child.

What aspects of their childbirth experiences were similar?

What aspects of their childbirth experiences were different?

What suggestions could they give you to prepare for the birth of a baby?

What did you learn from this experience?

REFLECTION

Making a Birth Plan

Prospective parents must make any important decisions, and the more informed they are, the better able they will be to decide what is right for them. If you were planning a birth, which of these questions would be important to you? Look over this list, fill in your responses, and note which questions you would want to discuss with your doctor or nurse-midwife. Be sure the setting you choose (traditional labor and delivery room, alternative birth center within the hospital, or birth center) and the person you choose (doctor or nurse-midwife) would offer the services and facilities that you desire.

Admission

_____ What type of childbirth training do you encourage patients to take?

_____ I would like my coach to remain with me throughout the labor and delivery.

_____ I desire more than one person present during the delivery.

_____ I desire the option (if health permits) to walk during labor.

Labor

_____ Do you recommend intravenous fluids be started? When?

_____ What pain medications do you commonly use?

_____ At what point during the delivery do you use pain medications?

_____ If I desire more or less pain medication during my delivery, what might you say?

_____ What types of monitoring (internal or external) do you recommend?

Delivery

_____ I would like my delivery to take place at _____ (a hospital, an alternative birth center in hospital, a birthing center, home).

_____ If you are not available, who will deliver the baby? (If this occurs, will my birth plan be honored?)

_____ What percent of your deliveries are done by C-section?

_____ What are your feelings on doing an episiotomy?

_____ I would like my partner to stay with me throughout the birthing process.

_____ I would like _____ (friends, other relatives, children) present during labor or delivery.

_____ Can we use a camera or videotape during labor and delivery?

The Baby

_____ I want/don't want my baby boy circumcised. Is anesthesia used for this procedure?

_____ I desire immediate bonding with my baby, no matter what type of delivery occurs.

_____ I desire to nurse my baby immediately.

Recovery

_____ I desire my baby to room in with me.

_____ I do/do not want supplemental feedings for my child.

_____ What are the hospital's/center's procedures for visitation?

_____ Assuming there are no complications, how long after giving birth would I remain in the hospital?

_____ What kind of follow-up care is available?

REFLECTION

Ethical and Social Issues of Reproduction

The topic of reproduction technology is charged with feelings and conflict. How do you feel about the various issues listed below? (You may wish to place each issue on the continuum.)

10	9	8	7	6	5	4	3	2	1

Highly unethical   Neutral   Highly ethical

1. Fetal diagnosis

2. Abortion

3. Cesarean section

4. Older motherhood

5. Surrogate motherhood

6. Donor sperm

7. Intrauterine insemination and in vitro fertilization

8. Human cloning

Who should pay for any of the above (insurance company, government, individual)?

How much money would you be willing to spend in order to achieve a pregnancy?

REFLECTION

Life Without Children

Roughly 6% of married women in their childbearing years who are able to have children do not intend to. These marriages without children are now referred to as "childfree" rather than "childless." The following questions will give you a chance to reflect on your ideas and feelings about having children.

It has been suggested that we live in a "pronatal" society where attitudes and policies encourage parenthood for everyone. What are some of the messages you have gotten from society about having children?

For a week, take note if radio and television commercials or print advertisements give a pronatal message. When you watch television this week, notice any pronatalism in the shows.

Listen to conversations around you. Do you hear any pronatal messages when people talk? (For example, "It's so exciting, she's pregnant," or "I can't wait till you have children.")

What is our society's attitude toward couples who don't have children?

How would you feel about having a marriage/partnership without children?

GENDER AND SEXUAL IDENTITY QUESTIONS

Parenthood, Pregnancy, and Infertility

The first group of statements below concerns your views of parenthood and are applicable to everyone. The other statements concern pregnancy, childbirth, and infertility. Answer those that are relevant to you.

- When I think about being a parent I feel . . .

- When I'm around babies I feel . . .

- When I'm with little children I feel . . .

These questions are for those of you who have experienced childbirth or infertility. Answer the questions that are relevant to you.

Females

- I have had to deal with infertility and that has made me feel . . .

- During my pregnancy I felt . . .

- My feelings about my body during pregnancy were . . .

- The childbirth experience has affected me by . . .

- During my pregnancy and childbirth my relationship with the baby's father . . .

- After my pregnancy, my sexuality was affected by . . .

- Our relationship has been affected by the birth of the baby by . . .

Males

- I have had to deal with infertility and that has made me feel . . .

- During the pregnancy I felt . . .

- My feelings about my partner's body during pregnancy were . . .

- The childbirth experience has affected me by . . .

- During the pregnancy and childbirth my relationship with the baby's mother . . .

- After the pregnancy, our sexuality was affected by . . .

- Our relationship has been affected by the birth of the baby by . . .

During my second semester of college, I realized I was pregnant. The father of the baby was my boyfriend and now my husband. When I found out I was pregnant, my whole world fell apart. My dreams of finishing college and the possibility of getting a volleyball scholarship were crushed. It was definitely the most important and serious event in my whole life. It was hard for me to accept how much my life was going to change. Abortion was not an option for me; I never even considered it although my husband (boyfriend at the time) would have liked me to. I felt very much at peace the moment I realized I really had no other choice but to keep my baby and take care of him. I lived through a lot of embarrassment, I lost some friends, I lost (my boyfriend) for a while, but I was happy with my decision.

—33-year-old Caucasian female

My pregnancy was an amazing experience. Watching my body change and feeling this life moving and kicking inside of me was incredible. My husband and I took a Lamaze class, and it really helped prepare us for what was ahead. While it was still a painful experience, having my husband there and sharing the birth of our son is an experience we will never forget, and truly a miracle.

—28-year-old African American

CHAPTER 13
THE SEXUAL BODY IN HEALTH AND ILLNESS

LEARNING OBJECTIVES

At the conclusion of Chapter 13, students should be able to:

1. Define and describe the principal eating disorders and their origin, relationship to sexuality, and prevention and treatment.

2. Describe the effects of alcohol and drugs on sexuality, including their use as disinhibitors, effects, and relationship to sexual risk taking.

3. Discuss issues of sexuality and aging, especially menopause for women and slower sexual responses for men.

4. Discuss issues of sexuality and disability with reference to the special needs of those with physical limitations, chronic illness, and developmental disabilities.

5. Discuss issues of sexuality and cancer for women, including its detection, treatment, and psychological impact.

6. Discuss issues of sexuality and cancer for men, including its detection, treatment, and psychological impact.

7. Discuss women's sexual health issues, including toxic shock syndrome, endometriosis, and lesbian health issues.

8. Discuss the practice of female circumcision, including the process, prevalence, effects, and cultural issues.

9. Discuss prostatitis and its detection, treatment, and psychological impact.

10. Discuss the impact of DES on the daughters and sons of women who took it.

11. Recognize and define the key terms listed below.

Key Terms

eating disorders
anorexia nervosa
bulimia
binge eating disorder
climacteric
menopause
hot flash
osteoporosis
hormone replacement
    therapy (HRT)
benign prostatic hypertrophy
retrograde ejaculation

diabetes mellitus
benign tumors
malignant tumors
mammograms
fibrocystic disease
cervical dysplasia, also called
    cervical intraepithelial
    neoplasia (CIN)
Pap test
biopsy
oophorectomy
hysterectomy

androgen replacement therapy
prostate-specific antigen (PSA) test
toxic shock syndrome (TSS)
endometriosis
prostatitis
diethylstilbestrol (DES)
disinhibition
aphrodisiacs
clitoridectomy, also called
    female circumcision
infibulation

PRACTICE TEST QUESTIONS

(For answers see Part IV of this book.)

Multiple Choice

1. Which of the following is often associated with having an eating disorder?
   a. traumas rising from sexual abuse
   b. frequent masturbation during childhood
   c. a history of punishment for sexual exploration or interest
   d. a history of STDs

2. Which of the following describes the central feature of the condition known as anorexia nervosa?
   a. An individual has no interest or concern about food.
   b. A person takes great pleasure in having continuous hunger pangs.
   c. An individual becomes obsessed with pursuing greater levels of thinness.
   d. A person consumes large amounts of nonnutritional food such as fiber.

3. Effects of menopause often include all of the following EXCEPT:
   a. periods of intense warmth and flushing known as hot flashes.
   b. increased vaginal lubrication.
   c. loss of bone mass.
   d. thinning of the vaginal walls.

4. Normal sexual changes experienced by men in their forties and fifties usually include all of the following EXCEPT:
   a. achieving erections requires more stimulation.
   b. frequency of sexual activity declines.
   c. sexual interest and enjoyment decrease greatly.
   d. the amount of ejaculate and the force of ejaculation is less.

5. Gay men, lesbians, and heterosexuals are similar in that as they age:
   a. those with a strong commitment to their relationship are the happiest.
   b. sexual variety become more important.
   c. resentment and power often replace intimacy.
   d. sexual passion and desire usually disappears.

6. Women with spinal cord damage:
   a. lose all interest in sex.
   b. gradually develop multiple sclerosis.
   c. menstruate and can become pregnant.
   d. eventually fully recover the ability to have vaginal and clitoral orgasms.

7. The effects of diabetes on sexuality:
   a. are more negative for women than for men.
   b. dramatically affect fertility for men.
   c. often include erectile dysfunction.
   d. include loss of desire for sex by most diabetic women.

8. The following are guidelines for survivors of heart attacks to follow EXCEPT:
   a. resume sexual activities gradually.
   b. do not engage in sexual activity before or after vigorous exercise.
   c. avoid sexual activity if the weather is especially hot or cold.
   d. avoid having orgasms with any sexual activity.

9. Joe is 60 and suffering from an urgent and frequent need to urinate. He is most likely afflicted with
   a. retrograde ejaculation.
   b. prostatic hypertrophy.
   c. fibrocystic disease.
   d. fibroadenoma.

10. All of the following are associated with a higher risk of breast cancer EXCEPT:
    a. family history of cancer.
    b. history of breast cancer in a close blood relative (mother, sister, etc.).
    c. having small breasts.
    d. late childbearing.

11. Osteoporosis refers to:
    a. beginning stages of ovarian cancer.
    b. beginning of menopause.
    c. loss of bone mass.
    d. lowered production of estrogen.

12. All of the following are true about prostate cancer EXCEPT:
    a. it is common in men under 40.
    b. it is the most common form of cancer among men.
    c. it can be checked for by having a physician do a digital/rectal exam.
    d. there is a blood test to help in diagnosing it.

13. Testicular cancer:
    a. has been decreasing in rate.
    b. is most common among young white men between 20 and 35.
    c. can be detected only by a blood test.
    d. has a very low cure rate.

14. The daughters of women who were prescribed DES (diethylstilbestrol) have greater vulnerability to:
    a. uterine, breast, ovarian, and vaginal cancer.
    b. pelvic inflammatory disease.
    c. premature births.
    d. endometriosis.

15. Alcohol use can put people at high risk for:
    a. unwanted intercourse.
    b. sexual violence.
    c. acquiring sexually transmitted diseases.
    d. all of the above

True/False

Mark T or F on the line before the statement.

_____ 1.   Ambivalence toward their body and their sexual nature is often found in people with eating disorders.

_____ 2.   Most women require extensive medical treatment to help overcome the problems associated with menopause.

_____ 3.   People with disabilities still have sexual feelings.

_____ 4.   Women with spinal cord injuries can't get pregnant.

_____ 5.   A man who has had a spinal cord injury can father a child.

_____ 6.   Hormone replacement therapy is recommended for all women who go through menopause.

_____ 7.   Mammograms are recommended only if a woman has a history of breast cancer in her family.

_____ 8.   Anabolic steroids can cause a decrease in sperm production.

_____ 9.   A Pap test is used to detect breast cancer.

_____ 10. Prostate cancer has a high cure rate.

Fill-In

Choose the correct term from the list at the end of the section.

1.   The eating disorder characterized by episodes of binge eating and purging is known as _____.

whereas _____ is the eating disorder characterized by a "relentless pursuit of excessive thinness."

2.   A painful gynecological problem that involves uterine tissue spreading to other parts of the abdomen is

_____.

3.   The complete cessation of menstruation is called _____.

4.   The loss of bone mass caused by lowered estrogen levels is known as _____.

5.   The administration of estrogen, often combined with progestin, to deal with the symptoms of menopause is

known as _____ therapy.

6.   Tumors can be either _____, which means they are non-malignant, slow developing,

and localized, or _____, which means they invade other tissue and disrupt the normal functioning of vital organs.

7. For early detection of breast cancer, the American Cancer Society recommends that all women

   over 20 perform _____ once a month, and by age 50 should have an annual

   _____, which is a low-dose X-ray screening.

8. Treatments for breast cancer include the removal of the breast known as _____ and

   removal of just the tumor and lymph nodes, which is known as _____.

9. The most reliable means of making an early detection of cervical cancer is the _____,
   which is done during a pelvic exam and involves scraping cells from the cervix for examination.

10. The surgical removal of the uterus is known as _____, and is often considered an
    overdone surgery.

11. An infection that allows staph bacteria to multiply in the vagina and has been attributed to the use of tampons

    is _____.

12. An inflamed prostate gland is otherwise termed _____.

13. The phenomenon of activating normally suppressed behaviors that applies to alcohol and sex is known as

    _____.

anorexia nervosa	malignant
benign	mammogram
breast self-examination	mastectomy
bulimia	menopause
disinhibition	osteoporosis
endometriosis	Pap test
hormone replacement therapy (HRT)	prostatitis
hysterectomy	toxic shock syndrome (TSS)
lumpectomy	

Short Answer

1. What type of physical and psychological concerns do women have as they go through menopause? What approaches does the book suggest for treating the physical and psychological symptoms?

2. As we age we are more likely to be affected by the chronic illnesses of diabetes, cardiovascular disease, and arthritis. How can these diseases affect sexuality? What can those affected do to continue the expression of their sexuality?

3. What are some of the concerns regarding people with developmental disabilities and their sexuality?

4. What two things can women do to detect breast and reproductive cancers? What can men do to detect prostate cancer?

REFLECTION

Assessing Your Body Image

	Never	Sometimes	Often	Always
1. I dislike seeing myself in mirrors.	0	1	2	3
2. When I shop for clothing I am aware of my weight; consequently I find shopping for clothes somewhat unpleasant.	0	1	2	3
3. I'm ashamed to be seen in public.	0	1	2	3
4. I prefer to avoid engaging in sports or public exercise because of my appearance.	0	1	2	3
5. I feel somewhat embarrassed by my body in the presence of someone of the other sex.	0	1	2	3
6. I think by body is ugly.	0	1	2	3
7. I feel that other people must think my body is unattractive.	0	1	2	3
8. I feel that my family or friends may be embarrassed to be seen with me.	0	1	2	3
9. I find myself comparing myself with other people to see if they are heavier than I am.	0	1	2	3
10. I find it difficult to enjoy activities because I am self-conscious about my physical appearance.	0	1	2	3
11. Feeling guilty about my weight problem preoccupies most of my thinking.	0	1	2	3
12. My thoughts about my body and physical appearance are negative and self-critical.	0	1	2	3

Now, add up the number of points you have circled in

each column: _____   _____ + _____ + _____ + _____

Score Interpretation

The lowest possible score is 0 and this indicates a positive body image. The highest possible score is 36 and this indicates an unhealthy body image. A score higher than 14 suggests a need to develop a healthier body image.

In the space provided, draw (1) your body and (2) your perception of an ideal body of a person of your gender.

         (1) My body   (2) My idea of the ideal body

What differences do you see between your drawing of your own body and that of your ideal?

Where do your ideas about an ideal body come from?

List five positive things about your body.

1.

2.

3.

4.

5.

_____

Questionnaire used with permission. J. D. Nash. 1986. *Maximize Your Body Potential* (Palo Alto, Calif.: Bull Publishing).

OBSERVATION

Looking for the Perfect Body

The media sends us many messages about standards of beauty. These images can influence how we feel about our own bodies. In different eras or different cultures, the standards of beauty have varied. There have been cultures and times where heavy women were considered the most beautiful. Today the trend is to ultra-thin models. Look through magazines and cut out pictures of both men and women. (You may want to use them to make a collage to share with your class.) Answer these questions about the pictures.

Female pictures:

Does there seem to be an ideal body type?

What are the characteristics of that body including:
      breast size
      type of figure
      age
      ethnicity
      other

Do any models have bodies that suggest anorexia?

Male pictures:

Does there seem to be an ideal body type?

What are the characteristics of that body including:
      chest size
      facial and body hair
      type of figure
      age
      ethnicity
      other

Do any of the males have bodies that suggest steroid use?

Do you feel looking at these ads influences how you feel about your body and your sexuality? Remember the effect these images have on us is not always something we are conscious of.

Jane Pratt, the editor of *Sassy,* a magazine for teenage girls, has said that the recent trend to thinner models has led to more girls wanting to diet. Show a teenage girl the pictures you have collected and ask her what she thinks is the ideal body.

REFLECTION

The Unkindest Cut

The customs of clitorectomy, female circumcision, and infibulation are discussed in your textbook. Do you think people in our country should actively try to prevent this from going on in other countries or among certain groups in our country?

How would you react if a friend shared with you that this procedure (female circumcision) had been done to her?

How would you react if this friend also told you it was the custom of her country and she felt it should be done to her daughters also?

How would you answer the argument that things we do in our country (breast implants, male circumcision) might be considered mutilating, barbaric, and unnecessary surgeries by people from other cultures?

OBSERVATION

The Disabled and Sexuality

The disabled are usually treated in the media as if they are not sexual. However, there are some movies that have explored the subject. Rent and watch the movie "Coming Home," "Scent of A Woman," or "My Left Foot" and answer these questions.

Was the person with the disability shown having sexual feelings?

How did the person handle his or her sexual feelings?

How did others react to this person's sexual feelings?

Were there any differences in how they dealt with sexuality compared to someone without a disability?

Did the movie change your view of sexuality and disability? If so, how was it changed? If not, how was it reinforced?

GENDER AND SEXUAL IDENTITY QUESTIONS

Body Image and Health

Answer the questions that are relevant to you.

- Society's emphasis on weight and beauty has affected me by . . .

- I had an eating disorder when . . .

- I dealt with it by . . .

- My sexuality is affected by my feeling about my body when . . .

- When I think about my body aging I feel . . .

- I have had my health interfere with my sexuality when . . .

- The effect(s) of drugs and/or alcohol on my sexuality has/have been . . .

Females:

I do/do not do breast self-examination because . . .

Males:

I do/do not do testicular self-examination because . . .

Dealing with cancer has had an effect on my sexuality. I used to have long, beautiful, blonde hair but as I write this I am bald from chemotherapy. I was not at all prepared for losing my looks and along with that much of my sexual identity. It has taken me by surprise to realize how much the way you look influences how people react to you, especially the opposite sex. Since I was diagnosed with cancer I have felt such a betrayal from my body.

—32-year-old Caucasian female

At the age of 36, I was diagnosed with breast cancer and had a breast removed. At that time I was not as concerned with the way that I would look as I was with the chance that I might die from this thing eating me away. My husband has always been there for me through all of the years we have dealt with this, as has my son. I never felt that anyone was repulsed by my changed body, but rather was concerned that I was well and there with them. I never felt that my breast was the only part of me that was important to my husband, nor was it the thing that made me a woman. Our sex life didn't change at all as a result of the loss of the breast, and in comparing the time before I had reconstruction to the time after, I think that there was really no appreciable difference attributable to my having or not having two breasts. There has certainly been no negative change in my attitude. If anything, I may enjoy sex even more knowing how precious each moment of life is.

—45-year-old Caucasian female

There are so many things that have affected my sexual identity—my diabetes, my eating disorder, my negative body image, and this underlying pressure of having to be perfect. *It is my own pressure; I can't keep blaming people or things. I have to fix it!*

—27-year-old Caucasian female

CHAPTER 14
SEXUAL ENHANCEMENT AND THERAPY

LEARNING OBJECTIVES

At the conclusion of Chapter 14, students should be able to:

1. Discuss the basis of sexual enhancement programs and the role of self-awareness, including conditions for "good" sex and "homework" exercises.

2. Describe ways of intensifying erotic pleasure, including the role of arousal and replacing coitus with erotic activities.

3. List the phases of Kaplan's tri-phasic sexual response model and identify the disorders or dysfunctions associated with each phase.

4. Identify sexual disorders and describe hypoactive sexual desire and sexual aversion.

5. Describe the major male sexual dysfunctions, including erectile dysfunctions and inhibited, delayed, or premature ejaculation.

6. Describe the major female sexual dysfunctions, including vaginismus, dyspareunia, and anorgasmia.

7. Discuss the physical causes and treatments of sexual dysfunctions for women and men, including devices for men with erectile difficulties.

8. Discuss with examples the psychological causes of sexual disorders and dysfunctions, including immediate causes, conflicts with oneself, and relationship causes.

9. Describe the treatment of sexual difficulties through cognitive-behavioral, psychosexual, PLISSIT, self-help, and group therapy approaches.

10. Identify considerations in choosing a sex therapist, including unique considerations for gay men and lesbians.

11. Recognize and define the key terms listed below.

Key Terms

sexual enhancement	priapism
sexual dysfunctions	vaginismus
sexual disorders	dyspareunia
hypoactive sexual desire (HSD)	anorgasmia
inhibited sexual desire	pubococcygeus
sexual aversion	sex surrogates
erectile dysfunction	sensate focus
premature ejaculation	PLISSIT model
inhibited ejaculation	erotic aids
Peyronie's disease	Kegel exercises

PRACTICE TEST QUESTIONS

(For answers see Part IV of this book.)

Multiple Choice

1. Sexual enhancement:
   a. is the same as sex therapy and is used to treat couples with dysfunctions.
   b. deals mainly with the mechanics of sex.
   c. refers to programs for people who function well sexually, but feel they can improve the quality of their sexual interactions and relationships.
   d. is used to increase the size of the penis.

2. While making love, Richard often finds himself observing himself and his partner and evaluating "how well" things are going. This distraction often leads to lack of orgasm. This behavior of judging performance is called:
   a. inhibited orgasm.
   b. spectatoring.
   c. anorgasmia.
   d. sensate focus.

3. Treatment for hypoactive sexual desire (HSD):
   a. requires the patient to stop masturbating.
   b. is easier and quicker than the treatment for other sexual dysfunctions.
   c. usually requires psychosexual therapy.
   d. involves taking specific drugs.

4. Which of the following is the newest and is becoming the most popular treatment for erectile dysfunctions?
   a. injections of medication into the penis
   b. a pill you take one hour before you want an erection (Viagra)
   c. suction devices
   d. penile implants

5. Primary erectile dysfunction:
   a. means a man has never had an erection.
   b. means a man has had erections in the past, but can't have them now.
   c. means that a man can have erections, but can't ejaculate.
   d. none of the above

6. John and Mary want to have intercourse but when they try the muscles around her vaginal entrance go into contractions so John can't insert his penis. Mary probably has the condition known as
   a. anorgasmia.
   b. dyspareunia.
   c. sexual aversion.
   d. vaginismus.

7. The most common female dysfunction seen by sex therapists is:
   a. vaginismus.
   b. dyspareunia.
   c. anorgasmia.
   d. sexual aversion.

8. Sexual dysfunctions
   a. can be caused by physical or psychologically factors.
   b. are always psychologically caused.
   c. usually disappear spontaneously.
   d. are always physically caused.

9. Psychological causes of sexual dysfunctions include all the following EXCEPT:
   a. fatigue and stress.
   b. sexual anxieties.
   c. relationship conflicts.
   d. poor blood circulation.

10. The Masters and Johnson approach to treating sexual dysfunctions:
    a. stresses a purely psychosexual therapy approach.
    b. works with only the affected individual.
    c. works with the couple involved.
    d. is the same as the PLISSIT model.

11. Ron and Esther are having marital problems, and among them are sexual problems. He feels Esther is too demanding sexually. She feels dissatisfied and not considered in their lovemaking. He feels anxiety about her complaints that he reaches orgasm too quickly for her to enjoy herself at all. Most likely, Ron's problem is one of
    a. premature ejaculation.
    b. erectile dysfunction.
    c. dyspareunia.
    d. inhibited ejaculation.

12. As quoted in the textbook when discussing the treatment of anorgasmia in women, "The main principle of achieving orgasm is simple: maximize the _____ and minimize the _____."
    a. stimulation, inhibition
    b. pressure to clitoris, pressure to breasts
    c. music, stress
    d. orgasm, resolution

13. Which sexual dysfunction is NOT frequently viewed as a problem by lesbians, but is by some heterosexual women?
    a. aversive feelings toward cunnilingus
    b. aversion toward anal eroticism
    c. anorgasmia
    d. homophobia

14. Jerry and Beverly begin lovemaking, but Jerry is unable to get an erection. He has the dysfunction known as:
    a. erectile dysfunction.
    b. premature ejaculation.
    c. inhibited ejaculation.
    d. delayed ejaculation.

True/False

Mark T or F on the line before the statement.

_____ 1. Suction devices to treat erectile dysfunction are seldom effective.

_____ 2. Gay men and lesbians do not experience sexual dysfunctions.

_____ 3. Masters and Johnson have found that religious teachings that stress guilt and negative feelings about sexuality can contribute significantly to sexual dysfunctions.

_____ 4. As we consider our sexuality, it is important to realize that sexual difficulties and problems are not that unusual.

_____ 5. The "squeeze technique" is used to treat vaginismus.

_____ 6. A mutually agreed-upon temporary ban of intercourse can enhance eroticism in a relationship.

_____ 7. Used as a treatment modality in sex therapy, sensate focus involves concentrating on touch and pleasuring.

_____ 8. Learning about your own body's responses through masturbation can often help with sexual problems.

_____ 9. Erotic aids such as vibrators are dangerous as people often get "addicted" to them.

_____ 10. Sexual aversion is experienced more by women than by men.

Fill-In

Choose the correct term from the list at the end of the section.

1. A consistent phobic response to sexual activity or the idea of such activity is known as

   _____.

2. Painful intercourse is known as _____.

3. The name of the sexual dysfunction where a woman does not have an orgasm is _____.

4. A treatment for premature ejaculation is to practice the _____.

5. Difficulty in controlling or delaying male orgasm is called _____.

6. The term given by Masters and Johnson to the process in which a person "looks on" and "judges" his or

   her own sexual performance is _____.

7. The term for the Masters and Johnson technique that emphasizes focusing on giving and receiving of

   pleasure by touch is _____.

8. The sexual dysfunction in women that is treated with vaginal dilators is _____.

9. The acronym name of a model of therapy for sexual dysfunction that has four progressive levels starting with permission giving is _____.

anorgasmia   sexual aversion
dyspareunia   spectatoring
PLISSIT   squeeze technique
premature ejaculation   vaginismus
sensate focus

Short Answer

1. What six conditions does the textbook suggest help contribute to "good sex"?

2. Briefly describe the Masters and Johnson approach to treatment of sexual dysfunctions.

3. Describe the four levels of the PLISSIT model of treatment of sexual dysfunctions.

 **OBSERVATION**

Finding Help

The textbook gives suggestions for what to look for in a sex therapist. Look under Psychologists and other mental health professionals in your local phone book and see if any advertise that they do sex therapy. Ask other professionals such as doctors or friends who they would recommend if someone has a sexual dysfunction.

Is it relatively easy to find sources?

What kinds of credentials or licenses do people who offer this kind of service have? Do any therapists mention that they belong to AASECT (American Association of Sex Educators, Counselors, and Therapists)?

Look for ads in newspapers, magazines, or Web sites that advertise help for men with impotence. (In many large newspapers, they advertise in the sports section.) Do these ads mention any credentials or licenses?

List five questions you might ask in order to assess a potential therapist's knowledge, experiences, and philosophy in treating sexual dysfunctions.

Sharing Intimate Sexual Feelings

Unfortunately, many couples are uncomfortable talking about intimate sexual feelings. Often we have grown up with the idea that sex just happens naturally, and believe that if the other person loves us they will know what pleases us. However, this is not true, and both men and women need to become more comfortable with sharing these feelings in their intimate relationships.

If you are not in an intimate relationship, review these questions and imagine what your reaction might be to discussing this with someone in your future. If you are in an intimate relationship, depending on how much you have communicated in the past, you might already know the answers to some of these questions. Look over this list, and see which ones you can answer. If you feel comfortable, use this list to start a conversation with your partner, and learn more about each other's feelings.

Does your partner like to have sex? How often?

What sexual positions does your partner like?

Does your partner like to have the lights on?

Does your partner like to be watched?

Does your partner like to talk or be talked to while making love?

What are your partner's feelings about the use of erotic aids or sex toys?

How important is cleanliness during sex?

What does your partner think of the smell and taste of your genital secretions?

Does your partner like to give and/or receive oral sex?

What does your partner think of your kisses?

As result of this experience, what did you learn about yourself? What did you learn about your partner?

 **REFLECTION**

Dealing with Dysfunctions

The textbook discusses sexual dysfunctions people may have over their lifetimes. What would you do if you or your partner were experiencing a dysfunction? Review the list below and check the option or options you think you would try.

FEMALE DYSFUNCTIONS

	Ignore it	Try self-help	Get professional help
Vaginismus	_____	_____	_____
Dyspareunia	_____	_____	_____
Primary anorgasmia	_____	_____	_____
Secondary anorgasmia	_____	_____	_____
Situational anorgasmia	_____	_____	_____
Hypoactive sexual desire	_____	_____	_____

MALE DYSFUNCTIONS

	Ignore it	Try self-help	Get professional help
Premature ejaculation	_____	_____	_____
Inhibited ejaculation	_____	_____	_____
Occasional erectile dysfunction	_____	_____	_____
Chronic erectile dysfunction	_____	_____	_____
Hypoactive sexual desire	_____	_____	_____

If the cause of erectile dysfunction was an injury or medical condition that would make it impossible for the man to have erections, which, if any, of these would you or your partner consider if the doctors felt they could be effective?

	YES	NO
Microsurgery to correct blood flow problems	_____	_____
Medications injected to cause temporary erections	_____	_____
Suction devices	_____	_____
Implants of penile prosthesis	_____	_____
Oral medication (Viagra)	_____	_____

 **REFLECTION**

Making Good Things Better

The textbook suggests that there are steps people can take to improve the quality of their sexual relationships. These include verbal and nonverbal communication, mirror examination, body relaxation and exploration, masturbation (also known as pleasuring), erotic aids such as vibrators, lotions, and videos, and a temporary ban on intercourse.

Which of these suggestions or exercises that can be done alone would you be comfortable doing?

Which of these suggestions or exercises would you be comfortable doing with a partner?

Which of these suggestions would you be less comfortable doing? Why?

GENDER AND SEXUAL IDENTITY QUESTIONS

Sexual Functioning

This chapter discusses how important psychological factors can be in causing sexual dysfunctions. Often early negative messages affect how we later feel about sexuality. Complete the statements that are relevant for you.

- I remember being caught "playing doctor" . . .

- From my parents' actions and words I learned that sex was . . .

- From religion the message I received about sex was . . .

- I first remember masturbating when . . .

- I have felt _____ about masturbation, probably because . . .

- I remember feeling guilty about sexual thoughts when . . .

- A concern I've had about my sexual functioning has been . . .

- When I have a sexual problem I feel . . .

- When I have a sexual problem I can discuss it with . . .

I played the drums in a rock band, which made me very popular with my peers. A negative consequence of that popularity was all the free drugs I received. Everyone wanted to get high with the band. I experimented at first with marijuana, cocaine, magic mushrooms, LSD, and PCP. Eventually I was using all these drugs frequently and sometimes together. My sexuality was affected as it lowered my inhibitions and caused me to make poor decisions regarding my partner choice. It also caused me to worry if there have been any negative effects on my reproductive system.

—26-year-old Caucasian male

There were may problems in the sexual aspect of our (my boyfriend's and my) relationship. Even though he was always very affectionate toward me, from the first time we tried to make love he was impotent. Even though he was able to have sex and achieve orgasm on a few occasions, most of our attempts at sex ended in failure. Eventually he lost the desire to even try. We just avoided sex altogether. Although he claimed it had nothing to do with me, it was hard not to take it personally and not to feel undesirable.

—22-year-old Caucasian female

My negative way to deal with what happened with my uncle and then my step-brother was to "tune out" the horrible memories and reactions to the sexual and physical abuse I had experienced by drinking and drugs and bulimia. Unfortunately this allowed me to be revictimized by bosses and a landlord until I was twenty-five and slowly started to get help.

—29-year-old female looking back at past sexual abuse

I knew of no one in my high school that was gay or even accepting of gays. I would come home every day and just cry because I knew I was gay and had no one to reach out to and talk about it with. I was scared to death. I felt like my life would always be unfulfilled and meaningless because of my sexual identity. I thought I would go through life watching people in love be together knowing I would never have that chance. I got so depressed that I tried to kill myself when I was seventeen because I was not like anyone else. I took a bunch of sleeping pills, but I got sick from them instead of dying.

—26-year-old Caucasian female remembering high school

Looking at Dad's magazines and movies was done in secrecy and privacy, usually when nobody else was around. My fear of being caught was due to embarrassment and fear of being yelled at. My parents never discussed mastur-bation. I remember my dad joking about it with a friend and how it could make you go blind. I never believed it. I suppose this comment and the fact that this was one subject they didn't talk to us about led to my choice of trying to diligently hide it. To this day I have never been caught in the act by my parents or my brothers.

—23-year-old Caucasian male

CHAPTER 15
SEXUALLY TRANSMITTED DISEASES

LEARNING OBJECTIVES

At the conclusion of Chapter 15, students should be able to:

1. Discuss societal ambivalence concerning STDs.

2. List and describe the social and biological factors contributing to the increase in the incidence of STDs.

3. List and describe the principal STDs (chlamydia, gonorrhea, genital warts, genital herpes, syphilis, hepatitis, urinary and vaginal infections, and parasitic infestations), including incidence, symptoms, and treatment.

4. Discuss the Tuskegee syphilis study and its impact on contemporary attitudes of African Americans toward public health agencies.

5. Discuss the impact of STDs on women, including "biological sexism," pelvic inflammatory disease (PID), and cystitis.

6. Discuss factors involved in STD prevention, including risk taking, abstinence, and safer sex.

7. Describe the components of the health belief model and give examples of each.

8. Recognize and define the key terms listed below.

Key Terms

incidence	nonspecific urethritis (NSU)	bacterial vaginosis
prevalence	syphilis	candidiasis
prophylaxis	genital warts	trichomoniasis
asymptomatic	human papilloma virus (HPV)	scabies
chlamydia	genital herpes	pubic lice
epididymitis	herpes simplex virus (HSV)	pelvic inflammatory disease (PID)
gonorrhea	prodrome	salpingitis
urinary tract infections	hepatitis	cystitis
nongonocccocal urethritis (NGU)	vaginitis	health belief model

PRACTICE TEST QUESTIONS

(For answers see Part IV of this book.)

Multiple Choice

1. Greg's job requires him to stay for several weeks at a time in many different cities. He sometimes engages in unprotected, casual sex during his visits. Greg has no worries about this, saying that he "feels just fine." Is there a problem here?
   a. No, while he is taking risks, he seems to be careful in his choice of partners.
   b. No, as long as he does this only occasionally, his risk is reduced.
   c. Yes, he should learn about the prevalence of STDs in the particular city he visits in order to judge his risk level.
   d. Yes, he may be without symptoms of an STD but nevertheless transmitting it to others.

2. Which of the following is NOT a factor that contributes to the transmission of STDs?
   a. STDs that are asymptomatic
   b. STDs that are airborne viruses
   c. development of a new resistant strain of STDs
   d. drug and alcohol abuse

3. Childbirth for a woman infected with genital herpes is complicated because:
   a. cervical cancer may prevent a vaginal birth.
   b. contact may cause serious infections of the eyes, mucous membranes, or nervous system.
   c. the infant will have herpes in his or her system for a lifetime.
   d. the infant's immune system is compromised.

4. Which of the following statements about chlamydia is true?
   a. It usually starts with a chancre.
   b. Most women show recognizable symptoms to chlamydia.
   c. It is the most common STD in the United States.
   d. It cannot be cured.

5. People who are sexually active with several partners:
   a. should get a screening for STDs if they notice symptoms.
   b. should get a screening for STDs if they think their partner has an STD.
   c. should get a screening for STDs every 3 to 6 months.
   d. should get a screening for STDs every 2 years.

6. For most sexually transmitted diseases:
   a. men and women are equally likely to have symptoms.
   b. men are more likely than women to have symptoms.
   c. women are more likely than men to have symptoms.
   d. only men and women over age 20 have symptoms.

7. The treatment for gonorrhea is usually:
   a. penicillin.
   b. laser therapy.
   c. podophyllin.
   d. acyclovir.

8. Which of the following is caused by exposure to human papilloma virus?
   a. chlamydia
   b. gonorrhea
   c. genital warts
   d. syphilis

9. What does your text mean by the "biological sexism" of STDs?
   a. Men are more likely to transmit STDs than are women.
   b. Men can more easily tell if their partners are infected with an STD.
   c. Women are more vulnerable to infection and the long-term effects of STDs compared to men.
   d. There are fewer barrier techniques available to women to protect them from STDs.

10. Which STD can be prevented by a vaccination?
    a. chlamydia
    b. hepatitis B
    c. gonorrhea
    d. syphilis

True/False

Mark T or F on the line before the statement.

——— 1. One of the factors that contributes to the high incidence of STDs in the United States is our ambivalence about sexuality.

——— 2. Genital warts are cured with penicillin.

——— 3. Genital herpes is caused by a bacteria.

——— 4. The drug that can help in reducing or suppressing herpes symptoms is acyclovir.

——— 5. A person with syphilis may not have any symptoms for years after contracting the disease.

——— 6. Vaginitis always occurs as a result of sexual activity.

——— 7. Barrier methods of birth control, like the diaphragm, provide more protection against STDs than the birth control pill.

——— 8. A person with a sexually transmitted disease will always have noticeable symptoms.

——— 9. The "Tuskegee experiment" is considered a model of how public health research should be done.

——— 10. The health belief model can help us better understand the role of denial in the transmission of STDs.

Fill-In

Choose the correct term from the list at the end of the section.

1. The technical name for the common yeast infection is _____.

2. A small red bump that often appears during the early stage of syphilis is called a _____.

3. A bladder infection that affects mainly women and is often related to sexual activity is

    _____.

4. The most prevalent STD in the United States and a primary cause of infertility and ectopic pregnancy is

    _____.

5. The STD that is sometimes called "the clap" or "drip" and that may manifest itself by causing painful

    urination and/or discharge is _____.

6. The viral STD that has symptoms which can range from being almost undetectable inside the vagina to

    appearing like miniature cauliflowers on the penis is _____.

7. Just prior to an outbreak of herpes is a period of a few days when the virus is active and shedding; this period

    is known as _____.

8. The sexually transmitted disease that starts with a chancre is _____.

9. The viral disease that affects the liver and can be sexually transmitted is _____.

10. A person who transmits an STD without any obvious signs or symptoms is said to be

_____.

asymtomatic   genital warts
candidiasis   gonorrhea
chancre   hepatitis
chlamydia   prodrome
cystitis   syphilis

Short Answer

1. What are two social and/or cultural factors that contribute to the spread of STDs?

2. Name and briefly describe two biological factors that contribute to the transmission of STDs.

3. Explain what is meant by "biological sexism," and give two reasons why it exists.

4. List three specific health behaviors that help protect us from STDs.

 **OBSERVATION**

Facts About Sexually Transmitted Diseases

Familiarize yourself with different types of sexually transmitted diseases by completing the chart below.

	Early signs and symptoms (in men and women)	Effects of long-term or untreated infection	Diagnosis and treatment
HIV infection (See Chapter 17)			
Hepatitis B			
Syphilis			
Chlamydia			
Gonorrhea			

	Early signs and symptoms (in men and women)	Effects of long-term or untreated infection	Diagnosis and treatment
Pelvic inflammatory disease (PID)			
Genital warts			
Herpes			
Trichomoniasis			
Candida albicans (yeast infection)			
Pubic lice			
Scabies			

REFLECTION

What's Your Risk?

There are many factors that influence your risk of getting an STD. Some of these are risk factors while others are risk markers. This can give you some idea of what your risk is of getting a sexually transmitted disease. Get out your calculator.

1. Begin with zero.

2. If your age is 11–15, add 5 points.

3. If your age is 16 or over, add 7 points.

4. Add 3 points for each sex partner during the last year.

5. Subtract 1 point for each partner you knew for at least 6 months before having sex.

6. Subtract 1 point for each partner with whom you discussed STDs and risk factors.

7. Subtract:

    3 points if you do or would use a condom with every sexual contact

    2 points if you would use a condom at least half of the time

    1 point if you would only use a condom sometimes

8. Subtract 2 points if you understand STD symptoms and would seek help immediately after identifying one.

Got your score? Here is how it can be evaluated:

Low risk	0–5
Moderate risk	6–10
Serious risk	11+

Answer these questions:

Did your rating compare with what you would have guessed?

Did you underestimate or overestimate what your risk would be? Why?

If your score is over 5, what could you do to bring it down? How would you feel about doing that?

Adapted from American Social Health Association, 260 Sheridan Ave., Palo Alto, CA 94306.

REFLECTION

Talking About STDs

The time to think about prevention is before you have sex. Caring about yourself and your partner means asking questions and being aware of signs and symptoms.

1. How do you define safer six?

2. List several ways to bring up the subject of STDs with a new partner. How would you ask whether or not he or she has been exposed to any STDs or engaged in any risky behaviors? (Remember that since many STDs can be asymptomatic it is important to know about past behaviors even if no STD was diagnosed.

3. How would you bring up the subject of condom use with your partner.

4. How might you convince someone who does not want to use a condom?

5. If you have had an STD in the past that you might possibly still pass on (e.g., herpes), how would you tell your partner(s)?

6. If you were diagnosed with an STD that you believe was given to you by your current partner, how would you begin a discussion of STDs with him or her?

7. How would you begin a discussion about your partner's past sexual history? What would you wish to know?

Talking about STDs may be a bit awkward, but the temporary embarrassment of asking intimate questions is a small price to pay to avoid contracting or spreading disease.

 **OBSERVATION**

Where to Go for Help

What types of resources are available in your community for the treatment of STDs? Where could you go, or send a friend who was worried and needed to be treated or get tested? Find out what types of services your college health clinic offers by calling and asking for the range of services and their prices. Also look in the telephone book to see what types of public services are available. Call one or two offices and inquire about the fees, services, and policy regarding anonymity and confidentiality.

After researching the alternatives, where would you go or send your friend?

Name of agency: Phone number:

Address:

Services:

Fees:

Why did you choose this facility?

Comments (for example, how it felt to call, attitude of people you talked to, etc.):

GENDER AND SEXUAL IDENTITY QUESTIONS

Sexually Transmitted Diseases

Having a sexually transmitted disease can definitely affect a person's self-concept and relationships. If this has happened to you or someone you have a sexual relationship with, examining your feelings by answering these questions can help you put the experience into perspective.

- I found out I had (name of STD) _____ when . . .

- I had/had not suspected that I had an STD because . . .

- My first reaction was . . .

- Later I felt . . .

- The first person I told was . . .

- I have/have not told anyone because . . .

- My feelings about sex changed/did not change since I found out because . . .

- I have found that telling people about it . . .

- My sexual partner told me that he/she had an STD when . . .

- It was before/after we had sex and so I felt . . .

- It changed/didn't change our relationship because . . .

- When (friend, relative) _____ told me he or she had an STD, I felt . . .

- It changed/didn't change our relationship because . . .

After little dating in high school, I went to college and immediately started a romance with a girl who was so attractive that I couldn't believe my luck. For three months I was on a cloud, but then I found out she was cheating on me. Not only that, she had left me a parting gift in the form of a sexually transmitted disease. I was devastated and my self-esteem was shot to hell. I was bitter and angry. I truly believed that such a bad thing would never happen to a guy like me, but actually I'm glad it did. The incident forced me to grow up and examine who I was, what I wanted, and what I needed from an intimate relationship with the opposite sex.

—25-year-old Asian male

What was I thinking? I had a few boyfriends throughout college, but I did not take my relationships seriously. Toward the end of college I had my last casual sex experience. Sadly I did not think twice about sleeping with those guys until I contracted on STD from the last one. The disease I contracted was genital warts, and it was horrible. The student health center on campus treated the warts with acid and did nothing else. After graduating, I moved and went to a private doctor. The warts were so bad that laser surgery was necessary. Unfortunately, I now have to go to the gynecologist twice a year because I am at a greater risk for cervical cancer because of the warts, number of sex partners, and sex at an early age.

—30-year-old Caucasian female

When I was fourteen, my grandfather talked to me about venereal disease. He explained to me about the types of sexually transmitted diseases and that the more sex partners I had the greater the risk of catching an STD. He told me to choose my partners carefully. He also said I should use condoms.

About two weeks later I met a girl. We decided that we wanted to be each other's first sex partner. I took my grandfather's advice and went to a drugstore and bought a box of Trojan condoms. My mom found out that I had sex. She was disappointed but was glad I used protection.

—23-year-old Caucasian male

CHAPTER 16
HIV AND AIDS

LEARNING OBJECTIVES

At the conclusion of Chapter 16, students should be able to:

1. List and describe the conditions and symptoms associated with HIV or AIDS.

2. Describe the principal components and functions of the immune system, the characteristics of the human immunodeficiency virus, and the process and progress of HIV infection.

3. Explain how HIV can and cannot be transmitted and discuss behaviors that put one at risk.

4. Discuss the effects of the AIDS epidemic on the gay community, including social, political, and psychological factors.

5. Discuss HIV/AIDS issues as they relate to women, children, adolescents, and older adults.

6. Discuss the AIDS epidemic in relationship to socioeconomic status and ethnicity.

7. Explain how to protect oneself against HIV infection and describe the principal types of HIV tests.

8. Discuss the issues surrounding HIV/AIDS education and prevention programs.

9. Describe the basic medical treatments for HIV and AIDS.

10. Discuss issues surrounding living with AIDS and caring for someone with AIDS, including discrimination and individual needs.

11. Recognize and define the key terms listed below.

Key Terms

human immunodeficiency virus (HIV)
acquired immune deficiency syndrome (AIDS)
opportunistic infections (OI)
pneumocystis carinii pneumonia (PCP)
Kaposi's sarcoma
wasting syndrome
leukocytes
macrophages
antigens
antibodies
lymphoctyes
B cells
helper T cells

killer T cells
suppressor T cells
reverse transcriptase
retroviruses
seroconversion
serostatus
parenteral transmission
perinatal transmission
cofactors
demographics
ELISA (enzyme-linked immunosorbent assay) viral load tests
protease inhibitors

PRACTICE TEST QUESTIONS

(For answers see Part IV of this book.)

Multiple Choice

1. The most common opportunistic infection of people with AIDS is:
   a. Kaposi's sarcoma.
   b. pneumocystis carinii pneumonia.
   c. tuberculosis.
   d. wasting syndrome.

2. All of the following groups presently show a rising rate of HIV infection EXCEPT:
   a. gay men.
   b. teenagers.
   c. women.
   d. injection drug users.

3. An important indicator of how the immune system is functioning is:
   a. the number of helper T cells.
   b. the number of killer B cells.
   c. the number of macrophages.
   d. the number of helper B cells.

4. HIV antibodies are usually detectable in the blood how soon after the virus enters the body?
   a. 2–6 hours
   b. 2–6 days
   c. 2–6 months
   d. 2–6 years

5. Opportunistic infections are diseases that:
   a. are not life threatening to people with HIV/AIDS.
   b. develop the same in healthy people as in people with HIV/AIDS.
   c. benefit from a vulnerable immune system.
   d. are favorable side effects that help fight HIV/AIDS infections.

6. Which form of sexual interaction presents the most risk for spreading HIV among men and women?
   a. anal intercourse
   b. vaginal intercourse
   c. oral sex
   d. all of the above are equally risky

7. Women with HIV:
   a. tend to be diagnosed earlier than men with the disease.
   b. have had more experimental drugs and medical treatments than men have had.
   c. often have to deal with issues of poverty and racism.
   d. are more likely to be lesbian than heterosexual.

8. In testing for HIV infection:
   a. the Western blot is given first and the ELISA is used to recheck positives.
   b. the ELISA is given first and the Western blot is used to recheck positives.
   c. the only test used now is the DNA-HIV.
   d. the DNA-HIV is given first and the ELISA is used to recheck positives.

9. Samantha and Ronald's daughter is in a day-care center with a child who has just been diagnosed with HIV. What should they do to ensure that their daughter will not be exposed to the virus?
   a. Nothing; transmission is highly unlikely in this casual environment.
   b. Move her to another day-care center immediately, after making sure none of the children there have HIV.
   c. Tell their daughter to avoid all contact with the child with HIV.
   d. Try to have the child with HIV removed from the day-care center.

10. How do most children contract HIV?
   a. infected breast milk
   b. perinatal transmission
   c. transfusions with infected blood
   d. child sexual abuse

11. The three basic types of medical treatments for HIV and AIDS include all of these EXCEPT:
   a. therapies to treat the symptoms and infections.
   b. drugs that affect the virus in some way.
   c. heat treatments that immobilize the virus.
   d. therapies that boost the immune system.

12. People with HIV and AIDS have faced discrimination:
   a. in housing.
   b. from medical caregivers.
   c. from courts and government agencies.
   d. all of the above

True/False

Mark T or F on the line before the statement.

_____ 1. The only difference between someone who is HIV-positive and someone who has AIDS is how long they have had the disease.

_____ 2. White fuzzy spots on the tongue are usually the first sign of HIV infection.

_____ 3. HIV can live and replicate in water.

_____ 4. HIV can be transmitted through oral sex between heterosexuals, gay men, or lesbians.

_____ 5. All children born to mothers who are HIV-positive will also be HIV-positive by age 2.

_____ 6. A person with HIV may be asymptomatic for years and unknowingly pass the disease to others.

_____ 7. Because they have strong immune systems, sexually active teenagers are at low risk for contracting HIV.

_____ 8. African Americans and Latinos are getting AIDS at a disproportionately higher rate than that of other Americans.

_____ 9. The number of helper T cells (called T4 count) in an individual's body is an important indicator of how well the immune system is functioning.

_____ 10. Public health officials estimate that by the year 2010, the numbers of women and men who test positive for HIV will be equal.

Fill-In

Choose the correct term from the list at the end of the section.

1. AIDs is an acronym for _____.

2. We call the diseases that take advantage of a weakened immune system _____.

3. The type of cancer that causes red or purple blotches to appear under the skin among those with AIDS is

   _____.

4. Large molecules that are capable of stimulating the immune system and then reacting with the antibodies that

   are released to fight them are called _____.

5. Viruses with the ability to reverse the normal genetic writing process are known as _____.

6. The process in which a person develops antibodies is called _____.

7. An HIV-infected person who has a sudden weight loss along with diarrhea and weakness is said to be

   suffering from _____.

8. Infection of HIV via the bloodstream is called _____.

9. Infection of HIV from a mother to a child in the womb is known as _____.

10. The most common simple blood test for HIV is called the _____ test.

acquired immune deficiency syndrome	parenteral transmission
antigens	perinatal transmission
ELISA	retroviruses
Kaposi's sarcoma	seroconversion
opportunistic infections	wasting syndrome

Short Answer

1. List four myths about ways that AIDS can be transmitted.

2. What reason is given for the shift in the epidemiology of HIV/AIDS?

3. What are three factors that put women at a higher risk for contracting HIV?

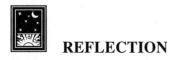

REFLECTION

Testing for HIV?

Your book discusses the feelings that people experience when they decide to get tested for HIV. There are two types of testing: anonymous and confidential. Anonymous testing is when you are identified only by a number. In confidential testing you provide your name, but there are strict laws that restrict access to that information.

Has reading this chapter changed your view on whether you need to be tested?

If you decided to be tested would you choose an anonymous or confidential test site? Why?

Look in a phone book, ask at your student health center, or call a hotline to find out where there is a test site in your area.

Look at the box entitled "An STD Attitude Scale" in Chapter 15 of this book. Does your decision to be tested or not agree with your rating? (People with moderate or serious risk should consider testing.) If it doesn't, how do you explain your decision?

If you have a friend who has had four partners over the last two years, including two that were "one-night stands," would you want that friend to be tested?

Do you think you could discuss this issue with that friend? If so, how might you approach him or her?

If you couldn't approach your friend, explain why.

Are you open to a discussion with a good friend regarding your getting tested?

 **OBSERVATION**

What's It Like to Buy Condoms at a Store?

One of the reasons that people don't use condoms is that they are embarrassed to buy them. Students have written that they drove over 50 miles to purchase condoms in a place where they would not be recognized. Others have said that the only thing they ever stole in their lives was condoms. (In fact, drug stores report that they are a frequently stolen item.) If doing this exercise alone sounds uncomfortable, try to find a classmate or friend to go with you.

Visit a drugstore and examine the various condoms. As you gather information, be aware of the feelings you are experiencing. If you are in an area with a condom specialty store like *Condomania,* you could visit that instead. (Another way to learn about and order condoms is over the Internet. Condomania has a homepage at http://www.condomania.com.) It's up to you whether you want to purchase condoms. If you do, you can add your reactions to the following list of questions.

Where in the store are the condoms displayed?

Is it a visible location? (Do you think people will easily find the display and then feel comfortable standing there?)

How are they packaged?

Does the packaging appeal to female as well as male buyers?

What types are available? (i.e., male, female, polyurethane, ribbed, lubricated, different sizes)

What is the range of prices?

Are foreign brands displayed?

How do you feel standing in the aisle looking at condoms?

If you bought any condoms, how did that feel?

 **REFLECTION**

HIV Prevention Attitude Scale

Complete the "HIV Prevention Attitude scale" located in the box in your textbook.

Do you feel it was an accurate measure of how positive your preventive attitudes are? Why?

Looking back over the statements, do you feel reading the chapter had any effect on your attitudes, or were they the same before reading the chapter?

If any attitudes have changed, to what do you attribute the change?

 **OBSERVATION**

Putting a Face on AIDS

The textbook discusses how outreach programs have people with HIV or AIDS speak to groups in order to personalize the HIV epidemic. If you have not heard such a presentation, renting the video "Common Threads—The Story of the Quilt" is a way to share a similar experience. If panels of the quilt come to your area, going to see them is another way to experience the personal side of this disease. You may also wish to access the story behind the quilt, images of the quilt panels, and information and links related to HIV infection, using the Web site titled "The Names Project Foundation AIDS Memorial Quilt" at http://www.aidsquilt.org. If you are able to do any of these or have had another personal experience with a person with AIDS or HIV, write your reaction here.

 **OBSERVATION**

Listening for AIDS Messages

Sensitizing oneself to an issue is a key factor in being able to understand and make decisions about that issue. For one week take note of every message about AIDS you see or hear in advertisements, news stories, on the radio and television, in movies, on the Web, and in conversation. Record them below:

Did you see or hear very much on the topic? (If not, and you would like more information, go to the Resource Center of your textbook and, using the Internet, look up some of the sites listed under HIV and AIDS.)

From what sources did you see or hear the most about AIDS?

If you knew that you were HIV-positive, how might you feel about what you heard or saw?

Do you feel that the media and public are sensitive to this issue?

After listening carefully over the last week, what can you say about your knowledge and feelings about this epidemic? Have they changed?

GENDER AND SEXUAL IDENTITY QUESTIONS

AIDS

- The first time I heard about AIDS was when I was about _____ years old. My first thoughts about it were . . .

- I thought the chances that anyone I knew would ever be affected were . . .

- When I heard that Rock Hudson, Magic Johnson, or (another famous person) _____ got AIDS I felt . . .

- As I got older my views about AIDS changed/did not change so that I now feel . . .

- I have known/not known anyone with AIDS and this has affected me by . . .

- AIDS has changed my life by . . .

- I have/have not been tested for AIDS because . . .

- To prevent AIDS I . . .

In the fall of 1985, my father became ill. He was hospitalized frequently, but the doctors did not know what was wrong. My father was a jolly man (he weighed about 268 lbs and stood 5'11"). During his last year, he lost significant amounts of weight. He was changing in front of our eyes not only physically but mentally as well. The disease that was taking over his body was taking over his mind and personality as well. He had become so debilitated that he could attend my high school graduation only for a short time and in a wheel chair. One week later he was taken to Stanford Medical Center where they diagnosed him with AIDS. He died five days later. This was so difficult and still is so difficult to deal with. My mother was astounded. She knew their relationship was not normal but had absolutely no idea he was gay. They had been married for 20 years and without a sexual relationship for 14 years. All that time my mom thought there was something wrong with her. My father led a hidden life. I may not have known his whole person, but the part of the man I knew, I loved. He was a great father. I miss him. I miss him so much!

—23-year-old Caucasian female

I am worried about AIDS because my doctor says that usually condyloma (which was recently diagnosed) is sexually transmitted. The pain I feel inside is overwhelming. The last and fourth time I had sex with him was in December, 1992. I had an AIDS test in February, 1993, and it came out negative. It should have made me feel better; however, it did not. The six-month window period will be over in June; however, I think that I am going to take one in May and in June, just to ease my heart.

—21-year-old African American female

CHAPTER 17
SEXUAL COERCION: HARASSMENT, AGGRESSION, AND ABUSE

LEARNING OBJECTIVES

At the conclusion of Chapter 17, students should be able to:

1. Discuss the issues surrounding the definition of sexual harassment, including the difference between flirtation and harassment.

2. Describe the different ways sexual harassment takes place in schools, colleges, and the workplace.

3. Discuss heterosexual bias and identify the sources of anti-gay prejudice, including religion, and how to decrease it.

4. Compare and contrast the different forms of sexual aggression, including acquaintance, stranger, marital, and gang rape.

5. Explain the impact of rape on its survivors, including rape trauma syndrome.

6. Describe the means of preventing sexual assault.

7. Identify the preconditions and forms of child sexual abuse, including characteristics of children at risk.

8. Describe initial and long-term effects of sexual abuse and sexual abuse trauma.

9. Discuss the principles involved in child abuse prevention programs and obstacles to implementation.

10. Discuss the debate over recovered (repressed) memories versus false memories as it applies to sexual abuse.

11. Recognize and define the key terms listed below.

Key Terms

sexual harassment
hostile environment
heterosexual bias (heterosexism)
anti-gay prejudice
homophobia
gay-bashing (queer-bashing)
rape
sexual aggression
date rape (acquaintance rape)
age of consent
statutory rape
rape trauma syndrome

posttraumatic stress disorder (PTSD)
secondary victimization
child sexual abuse
extrafamilial abuse
intrafamilial abuse
nonpedophilic sexual abuse
sexual abuse trauma
repressed memory
recovered memory
false memory
false memory syndrome

(For answers see Part IV of this book.)

Multiple Choice

1. Recent laws extending sexual harassment to include a hostile environment apply to:
   a. work situations at companies with more than 50 employees.
   b. work situations at all businesses regardless of the number of employees.
   c. the supervisor/employer, regardless of whether or not they were aware of the situation.
   d. b and c only

2. Sexual harassment is a mixture of sex and:
   a. flirting.
   b. telling dirty jokes.
   c. power.
   d. violence.

3. The factors that need to be examined to separate flirtation from sexual harassment include all of the following EXCEPT:
   a. whether you have equal power.
   b. whether you are approached appropriately.
   c. whether you wish to continue the contact.
   d. whether you are the more attractive person.

4. Dr. Smith sometimes tells off-color jokes in the classroom. These are usually about female body parts and bodily functions. He intersperses slide presentations with pictures of female nudes in provocative poses. Feedback to female students on their test papers often has sexual double entendres. This behavior may be considered sexual harassment through:
   a. requests for sexual favors.
   b. creation of a hostile environment.
   c. unwelcome sexual advances.
   d. physical conduct of a sexual nature.

5. If you are harassed by a professor or other college authority, what should be your first step?
   a. a clear statement to the harasser to stop the behavior
   b. a letter to the student newspaper
   c. an appointment with the harasser's supervisor
   d. taking steps to avoid any contact with the harasser

6. A broad term that refers to any kind of sexual activity initiated with another person through the use of argument, pressure, pleading, and cajoling, as well as force, pressure, alcohol or drugs, or authority is:
   a. sexual aggression.
   b. sexual coercion.
   c. acquaintance aggression.
   d. acquaintance rape.

7. Date rapes:
   a. are usually planned in advance.
   b. often involve the use of alcohol or drugs.
   c. seldom occur in fraternities, because others are around.
   d. are easily recognized by both participants as date rape.

8. Marital rape:
    a. is not recognized by law because it is not "real" rape.
    b. is a rare occurrence.
    c. leaves the victim experiencing betrayal, anger, humiliation, and guilt.
    d. is only recognized as a crime in Oregon.

9. The most brutal rapes in which sex and aggression are violently fused are usually:
    a. sadistic rapes.
    b. power rapes.
    c. anger rapes.
    d. date rapes.

10. Most victims of rape:
    a. probably led the other person on.
    b. experience depression, anxiety, restlessness, or guilt as a result of the rape.
    c. experience major physical injuries as a result of the rape.
    d. report the incident to the police.

11. Long-term effects of sexual abuse often include all the following EXCEPT:
    a. depression.
    b. self-destructive tendencies, including suicide attempts and thoughts.
    c. interpersonal relationship difficulties.
    d. less vulnerability to rape or marital violence because of increased awareness.

True/False

Mark T or F on the line before the statement.

_____ 1. When a husband forces his wife to have sex, it is not called rape.

_____ 2. Cultural and gender differences may contribute to confusion about what is sexual harassment.

_____ 3. Incidents of sexual harassment do not usually occur to a victim until their late teenage years.

_____ 4. The amount of violence toward gays has been exaggerated in the media, and is actually quite rare.

_____ 5. Heterosexual women tend to be more tolerant of homosexuality than heterosexual men.

_____ 6. The most common type of rape is acquaintance (date) rape.

_____ 7. The typical stranger rape involves an assailant who attacks a stranger in a public place in the dark.

_____ 8. Sexual assault against men may be perpetrated by other men or by women.

_____ 9. Almost all victims of child sexual abuse are females.

_____ 10. The most traumatic form of sexual victimization is believed to be father-daughter abuse.

Fill-In

Choose the correct term from the list at the end of the section.

1. The use of power for sexual ends or the creation of a hostile environment of a sexual nature is known as

   _____.

2. The tendency to see the world in heterosexual terms and to ignore or devalue homosexuality is known as

   _____, or heterosexism.

3. _____ is any kind of sexual activity against a person's will gained through the use of force, pressure, alcohol or drugs, or authority.

4. Sexual intercourse with a dating partner that occurs against his/her will and with force or the threat of force

   is known as _____ or _____.

5. Consensual sex with a female under the legal age of consent is known as _____.

6. Victims of rape often experience _____, which involves emotional changes an individual

   undergoes as a result of rape.

7. Any sexual interaction from fondling to genital penetration that occurs between an adult and a child is

   known as _____.

8. When sexual abuse occurs between biologically related individuals or step relatives, it is known as

   _____.

9. Violence directed against gay men or lesbians because of their orientation is known as

   _____.

10. Sexual intercourse between people too closely related to legally marry is defined as

    _____.

acquaintance rape	intrafamilial abuse
child sexual abuse	rape trauma syndrome
date rape	sexual aggression
gay bashing	sexual harassment
heterosexual bias	statutory rape
incest	

Short Answer

1. Imagine that you are asked to speak to incoming freshmen about sexual harassment. What information would you give them, and what advice would you offer to anyone who felt he or she was being sexually harassed?

2. What are the three main sources of anti-gay prejudice in individuals, and what are two characteristics of individuals who hold these beliefs?

3. Describe the two phases of rape trauma syndrome and their effects on the victim's sexuality. What steps can be taken to help in recovery?

4. What three factors put children at risk for sexual abuse? What are three of the most common effects that occur among victims of child sexual abuse?

 **OBSERVATION**

Does It Happen at Your School?—Rape

College campuses are prime sites for the occurrence of date rapes. As a result of increased media attention, campuses are now paying more attention by sponsoring educational meetings, as well as providing escort services, self-defense classes, and additional lighting at night. Find out what your campus is doing by contacting your Student Services, campus police, or student health services. As a result of your investigation, what did you learn?

Have there been any incidents of rape (including date rape) reported on campus in the last three years?

Was the person caught?

What was the outcome of the situation?

If there were any incidents, were they related to any specific groups such as athletic teams or fraternities?

If there were any incidents, was alcohol or drugs involved?

What services are available for people who have been victims of rape or harassment? (List both school and community resources.)

Find and keep a hot-line number that deals with this issue, so if you or anyone you know needs help you will know who to call.

 **OBSERVATION**

Does It Happen at Your School?—Harassment

Look in your school catalog or call someone in Student Services to find out what the official policy is for handling accusations of sexual harassment on your campus. Answer the following questions:

Is there an official policy?

What is that policy?

To whom is sexual harassment reported?

How is it followed up?

Would you file a report if you were sexually harassed?

Why or why not?

Have been any reported incidents of sexual harassment? If so, how many?

Who was involved? (i.e., student-faculty, student-student)

Has there been any anti-gay or anti-lesbian harassment reported?

If so, how was it handled?

What was the outcome for each case?

What was the attitude of the person you spoke to about sexual harassment on college campuses?

REFLECTION

Case History of a Date Rape: Paul and Susan

Who is responsible when a date rape occurs? Though this question may be obvious to most, upon re-examining the situation in which it occurred and hearing the stories of each person, some may question who is truly responsible. In this case, you decide.

Paul explains his story: I first met Susan at a dorm party. There she was, looking good in the tight black outfit she wore. We caught each other's eye and she gave me the sign that she was definitely interested. I approached her, we talked, danced, and I asked her if she would like to come to my room for a drink.

We talked for a while and it wasn't long before we began kissing. Soon, we were laying on my bed and I began to undress her. She put up a little resistance, like most girls do, but didn't seem that upset when I went under her dress. Then she finally stopped struggling and began to cry. I suppose she felt sad about something but I didn't want to get into anything with her.

She left soon afterwards. We didn't talk. I don't know why she should be so upset! We drank together, she came to my room, dressed and acted like she wasn't a virgin. So what's the big deal?

Susan's side of the story: A few of my girlfriends and I went to a party on Saturday night. I was feeling pretty good about myself and my life now that I'm finally away at college. A guy caught my eye and I thought he was kind of cute. We had a beer together, talked and danced. The noise and smoke made any kind of conversation difficult so I agreed to go to his dorm room so that we could talk.

We had another beer together and one thing led to another before I found myself kissing him. I didn't want him to get the wrong idea about me, since I only knew him for a short time, so I suggested we go outside for a walk. Since it was cold outside, he suggested it would be more comfortable at his place. The kissing was nice, but pretty soon, he got more passionate. I felt uncomfortable and began to push away. It was as though he didn't hear me! All of a sudden, his hand was under my dress, pushing away my underwear and grabbing at my genitals. I tried to push him away, and yelled at him to stop, but he wouldn't. I was scared and began to cry. He raped me.

A few minutes later, he was fast asleep. I got dressed and slipped out of his dorm. I don't ever want to see him again. Never in a million years did I dream this could happen to me.

After reading the case history, answer the following questions:

Who is wrong? Why?

Adapted from *Acquaintance Rape: Is Dating Dangerous?* Prepared by ACHA (American College Health Association), Baltimore, MD, 1987.

Who was responsible for what happened?

What situations/circumstances would you have changed?

What could Paul have done to prevent this from happening?

What could Susan have done to prevent this from happening?

What assumptions did each character hold which were stereotypical or incorrect?

Given what happened, what should Susan do?

 **REFLECTION**

The Line Between Harassment and Flirtation

Drawing the line between flirtation and harassment is not always easy and can be filled with ambiguity. Read over the following stories, and note whether you believe someone is being harassed.

1. Jack and Hillary work together at a law office. Jack tells Hillary she looks really great in her new dress, and later asks her out to dinner. She says no. He asks her out again the next week. And the following two weeks.

   Is this harassment?

   What should Hillary do?

   What would you do if you were Hillary?

2. Mike and Susan work together. Mike is constantly telling sexually explicit jokes to the other workers while Susan is around. He also keeps making compliments about Susan's figure. The last few days he has started to playfully pat her rear end, and tell her how cute it looks.

   Is this harassment?

   What should Susan do?

   What would you do if you were Susan?

Ask a friend or classmate of the other sex to do this same exercise and compare your answers.

What parts of your answers are the same?

What differences were there?

 **OBSERVATION**

Preventing Childhood Sexual Abuse

Scandals involving childhood sexual abuse have received a great deal of attention. Since these episodes and the public awareness they generated, there have been significant efforts made at prevention. In this activity you can assess the type and availability of education and materials in your community.

1. **Library** Find a book on prevention of sexual abuse written for children, such as *A Better Safe Than Sorry Book* by Sol and Judith Gordon. Read it or a similar book and answer the questions below. (These books are short and don't take long to read!)

   If you were a parent would you read this to your child?

   Would it make any difference if your child was a boy or girl?

   What age would be appropriate for introducing this concept to your child?

   How do you think you would have felt if this book was read to you at that age?

   Do you think this book might scare children, or have any negative effects on their sexual feelings?

2. **Video Store** Many video stores have the video for children to watch called *Strong Kids, Safe Kids*. It is aimed at preventing child sexual abuse and is moderated by Henry Winkler. Watch this video and answer the questions below.

   If you were a parent would you watch this video with your child?

   Would it make any difference if your child was a boy or girl?

   At what age would you want your child to watch this video?

   Do you think this video might scare children, or have any negative effects on their sexual feelings?

3. **Police Department** Call your local police department and see if they have any materials (some have "comic books") that they distribute for use with children. Read them and answer the questions under the Library section.

4. **Schools** Call your local school district and find out what types of education they provide about sexual abuse. If materials are available to view, review them and answer the questions under the Library section.

5. **Web site** Use the Resource Center of the text to locate and research a Web site that addresses child sexual abuse (i.e., *National Committee to Prevent Child Abuse:* http://www.childabuse.org or the *National Victim Center:* http//www.nvc.org/). Review the information and resources and adapt, as appropriate, the questions under the Library section.

GENDER AND SEXUAL IDENTITY QUESTIONS

Negative Experiences

One of the aspects this chapter deals with are the negative sexual experiences people can have. Sometimes it can be difficult to recognize and acknowledge that something that has happened was sexual abuse. Sometimes people try to deny these experiences, or they recall memories that are uncomfortable but they don't label it as sexual abuse. The problem with not acknowledging these experiences is that they can affect our sexuality in other ways. Regardless of whether we are male or female, dealing with the experience and the feelings we have from it can change us from a victim to a survivor. Answer the following questions that apply to you.

- When I was a child something that happened to me that I now recognize as sexual abuse was . . .

  At the time it happened the way I felt about it was . . .

  Now when I think about it I feel . . .

- I have been affected by sexual harassment when . . .

  At the time I realized/didn't realize it was harassment and so . . .

- I think that I have/have not been tricked into having sex when . . .

  At the time it happened I felt . . .

  When I think about it now I feel . . .

- I have/have not been forced into having sex when . . .

At the time it happened I felt . . .

When I think about it now I feel . . .

- My attitude toward gay, lesbian, and bisexual people is . . .

When I think about why I feel that way I think it is because . . .

The first time I can remember anything about the abuse, I must have been about five years old. The perpetrator was a member of my own family—an uncle by marriage. I seem to remember this man fondling me in front of his own children. Having no recollection of the abuse, I tried things with boys and girls never knowing why. I always felt disgusted and ashamed of my behavior and didn't tell a soul. I also had other cousins, both females and males, try things with me. I don't blame these particular individuals since they too were molested by the same individual. I now know as an adult that children (humans) learn through experience, and one can't reenact a situation that they have never experienced.

—27-year-old Hispanic female

As I got closer to the bed, (an acquaintance) Tom pushed me down. I was on my stomach lying on the bed while he was sitting on my back. I asked him, "What are you doing?" Still, I didn't feel any threat from him. Tom started to touch my body and said, "I want to f___ you." "What?" I replied. "Let me f___ you," he said. "No! I don't like doing that." He pulled my underwear down and began squeezing my butt. "Don't do that," I said. Then, he jammed his fingers into my anus. Boy, was it uncomfortable. I gave him a quick jolt and pushed him off me. I ran to the bathroom and locked the door. I was scared. Tom pounded on the door, pleading, "Let me in, let me touch you, I come very quick." When I look back at the incident, I felt like I was exploited of my rights, my privacy, and my security.

—24-year-old Vietnamese male

This very good friend of mine, I thought, walked me back to my dorm room. Shortly afterwards, he began holding me and kissing me in a romantic way. I went along with it because I was vulnerable, and I felt that he cared a great deal for me. Unfortunately, he began fondling me and slowly started removing my clothes. As he got down to my panties I realized that this was wrong, and I didn't want or like him in that way; so the terror began.

I was so afraid and unsure of what was going to happen so I said, "I don't want to do anything." Soon he began to get very angry, holding me down firmly and sucking my breasts. As he moved toward my crotch, I started crying and begged him to stop. He was so upset he started choking me and said, "You shouldn't let a guy take you that far because the next time it won't be this easy." I felt so embarrassed and humiliated. I was terrified of this person but never told anyone what had happened because I felt it was all my fault.

—23-year-old Black female

CHAPTER 18
COMMERCIAL SEX

LEARNING OBJECTIVES

At the conclusion of Chapter 18, students should be able to:

1. Distinguish the differences in meanings between sexually oriented material, pornography, and erotica.

2. Discuss changing perspectives about what constitutes pornography, including the role of deviance, moral outrage, and the significance of personal response.

3. Discuss the reasons people use sexually oriented material.

4. Evaluate arguments concerning the impact of sexually oriented material on behavior, especially aggression against women and gender discrimination.

5. Discuss child pornography, including its impact on children, laws against it, and debate about its extent.

6. Evaluate the arguments concerning the censorship of sexually oriented material, including legal issues revolving around obscenity, as well as popular music.

7. Discuss female prostitution, including motivation and types of prostitution.

8. Discuss male prostitution, including differences between delinquent and gay male prostitutes.

9. Discuss prostitution and the law, including decriminalization, regulation, and the HIV/AIDS epidemic.

10. Recognize and define the key terms listed below.

Key Terms

erotica	femme porn
pornography	censorship
obscenity	prostitution
sexually oriented material	peer delinquent subculture
sexually explicit material	she-male
hardcore	solicitation
softcore	

PRACTICE TEST QUESTIONS

(For answers see Part IV of this book.)

Multiple Choice

1. The difference between erotica and pornography:
    a. is clearly defined by the legal code.
    b. has to do with what kinds of sexual acts are shown.
    c. depends on how arousing the material is.
    d. appears to be a subjective judgment.

2. All of the following are true about the content of sexually explicit material EXCEPT:
   a. Regardless of the source, the themes are quite similar.
   b. Sexual encounters often take place between people who have just met, and they show no interest in developing a relationship.
   c. The most common themes are mutual respect, honesty, and eroticism.
   d. There is a trend toward movies with a more romantic view as they appeal more to women

3. Which one of the following statements about child pornography is accurate?
   a. Child pornography accounts for about 50% of all sexually oriented material.
   b. Most adults who regularly use pornography eventually become interested in child-focused material.
   c. The creators and distributors of child pornography have been actively pursued and prosecuted in the United States.
   d. Participation in the creation of such material seems to have few negative effects on the children involved.

4. Anonymous telephone sex provides the caller with:
   a. a sense of reality about the needs and desires of others.
   b. pseudo-intimacy and a sense of physical closeness.
   c. inexpensive yet honest feedback about sexuality.
   d. support and referral for sexual needs and desires.

5. People who read or view sexually explicit material:
   a. usually recognize it as fantasy.
   b. use it as a release from their everyday world.
   c. find that it may activate a person's typical behavioral pattern.
   d. all of the above may occur

6. Prostitutes:
   a. are more likely to be accepted by their conventional peers who often admire their chosen profession.
   b. separate sex as a physical act for which they are paid from sex as an expression of intimacy and pleasure.
   c. are as likely as anyone else to have been sexually abused as children.
   d. have been shown to have a relatively high self-concept.

7. Of the following, who is the most likely to have a pimp?
   a. adolescent girls and streetwalkers
   b. call girls and masseuses
   c. older prostitutes
   d. male prostitutes

8. When women describe the most attractive things about their lives in the prostitution subculture, they describe:
   a. the excitement of their lives.
   b. the attraction and intimacy they have with their pimp.
   c. the monetary and material rewards.
   d. the sexual fulfillment they feel.

9. The most numerous prostitutes are those who are:
   a. call girls.
   b. masseurs.
   c. those who work in brothels.
   d. streetwalkers.

10. The only sexual offense for which women are extensively prosecuted is:
    a. exhibitionism.
    b. sexual addiction.
    c. prostitution.
    d. fellatio.

True/False

Mark T or F on the line before the statement.

_____ 1. Studies indicate that the majority of people support the right of adults to possess sexually explicit materials.

_____ 2. Clear definitions exist between what is obscene and what is not.

_____ 3. There is little evidence to indicate that nonviolent sexually oriented material is associated with actual sexual aggression against women.

_____ 4. While the courts have continually opposed censoring sexually explicit material, a major exception is child pornography.

_____ 5. Child pornography has a vast and widespread audience.

_____ 6. In recent years the printed word has become legally protected as an established art form and means of expression.

_____ 7. Many women who accept money or drugs for sexual activities do not consider themselves to be prostitutes.

_____ 8. The laws to end and/or control prostitution have been quite effective in ending it.

_____ 9. Prostitutes do not appear to be at any higher risk for contracting HIV/AIDS than the general sexually active population.

_____ 10. In contrast to male delinquent prostitutes, gay male prostitutes engage in prostitution as a means of expressing their sexuality and making money.

Fill-In

Choose the correct term from the list at the end of the section.

1. The term derived from the Greek meaning a love poem and that describes a positive evaluation of sexually oriented material is _____.

2. The term that represents a negative evaluation of sexually oriented material is _____.

3. Photographs, videos, films, magazines, or books whose primary themes, topics, or depictions involve sexuality or cause sexual arousal are called _____ material.

4. Material that intimately depicts sexual activities or genitals is called _____ material.

5. Computer developments have led to a new form of pornography known as _____.

6. Erotic films catering to women or couples and that tend to avoid violence, are less male-centered, and are more sensitive to women's erotic fantasies are termed _____.

7. When the government, private groups, or individuals impose their moral or political values on others by

suppressing works, ideas, or images they deem offensive, it is called _____.

8. Though difficult to arrive at a legal definition, _____ is the state of being contrary to generally accepted moral standards.

9. The exchange of money, drugs, or services for sex is called _____.

10. The _____ subculture, an antisocial youth culture, is part of a delinquent street life characterized by male and female drug dealing and theft.

censorship	peer delinquent
cyberporn	pornography
erotica	prostitution
femme porn	sexually explicit
obscenity	sexually oriented

Short Answer

1. List and describe two problems that make it difficult to arrive at a legal definition of pornography.

2. List and briefly describe two ways that technology has transformed and extended the ways in which sexually oriented material is conveyed.

3. Describe three functions of sexually oriented material.

 **OBSERVATION**

Pornography or Obscenity—You Be the Judge

If you are not comfortable viewing erotica, then choose something you are comfortable with evaluating, i.e., *Cosmopolitan,* a romance novel, or beauty contest.

Choose a medium such as movies, videos, photographs, magazines, printed word, Web site, "virtual reality," or other source that sells or promotes sexually explicit materials. For a moment, become "clinical" when you review the material. As you respond to the questions below, keep in mind the following definitions:

pornography:	Sexually oriented material that is negatively evaluated
obscenity:	Material deemed offensive to "accepted" standards of decency or morality
softcore:	Non explicit sexually oriented material
hardcore:	Sexually explicit material that intimately depicts sexual activities or the genitals

Fill in the following:

Name of medium

Theme of material

Audience for which it is intended

What messages were sent?

How were these messages conveyed?

Was violence utilized?

If so, at whom was it directed?

How would you label this material (see definitions above)?

What potential effect might it have on its audience?

How did you feel about or respond to the material you observed?

REFLECTION

Ruling on the Legality of Sex for Profit

For a moment, imagine yourself a member of the United States Supreme Court. Given the definitions and discussion provided about sexually explicit material, think for a moment how you might vote on the following issues:

1. a minor (17-year-old male) posing nude for photographs to be displayed and distributed in a national magazine

2. a prostitute (24-year-old female) soliciting for business in her own surroundings (brothel or apartment)

3. a prostitute (24-year-old male) soliciting for business on a public sidewalk and using local hotels, cars, and/or back alleys to conduct his business in

4. providing funding for prostitutes in order that they can, regularly and without cost to them, be checked for HIV and other STDs

5. sexually explicit photographs or artwork exhibited in a metropolitan public art gallery

What criteria did you use to evaluate each of the above? If you were subjective, provided opinions based on your personal biases and experiences, then you are very much like those who judge and legislate.

If you had to classify your views as liberal, neutral, or conservative, how would you articulate yours? What factors and experiences do you feel have influenced your attitudes about sexually explicit materials?

GENDER AND SEXUAL IDENTITY QUESTIONS

Pornography

If your experiences involve the use of erotica and you feel that it has had a significant impact on your sex education, sexual fantasies, and/or sexual practices, then you may wish to complete the following questions and include this section as a component of your gender and sexual identity paper.

- The first time I saw pornography was when . . .

- My reaction was . . .

- I have/have not used sexually explicit material because . . .

- The primary medium I utilized to sexually stimulate or help to eroticize my sex life was . . .

- I used sexually explicit material when I felt . . .

- It helped to make me feel . . .

- From the materials, I learned . . .

- The most negative impact it has had on me is . . .

- The most positive impact it has had on me is . . .

- The influence that erotica or other sexually explicit material has had on my relationship with others . . .

My parents did not mind me looking at my father's Playboy. *In fact, at 16 they gave me my own subscription!*
—24-year-old Caucasian male reminisced about his exposure to pornography

She (my aunt) actually started molesting me when I was six. She would come home late at night, drunk, and carry me into her bed so that she could perform oral sex on me. She molested me until I was 12 years old. She was a prostitute so later in my molestation she tried to include her tricks, but I cried my way out of it every time.
—26-year-old African-Mexican-Native American female

(My friend) Richard's parents thought cartoons were too violent. His family answered the door naked, they were always naked if they were at home. I would watch pornographic movies on Select TV (movie channel) late at night. My friends and I would discuss sex all the time, yet most of our assumptions were wrong. I turned to pornography and friends to learn about sex as opposed to the institutions that were supposed to teach it.
—25-year-old Caucasian male

PART III

RESOURCES FOR READING AND WRITING
ABOUT HUMAN SEXUALITY

READING A JOURNAL ARTICLE

Academic journals are among the most reliable sources for information about human sexuality. The articles in such journals are scholarly and well-researched. Furthermore, the articles are generally reviewed by academic peers to ensure their scholarliness and accuracy. They should, nevertheless, be read critically as they may contain errors or inadequately substantiated conclusions. Chapter 2 of the textbook will help you critically evaluate articles.

If a journal or article is unavailable at your school's library, most libraries are now able to take advantage of services that make it possible to have articles faxed or sent. You may wish to check with your librarian early in the semester to see if this service is available. Many opportunities also exist to gather information through the World Wide Web. Many journals have Web sites that contain the table of contents from the journals, while others have abstracts or complete articles available. Check with your librarian and academic computing personnel to see if you have access to these resources. A commercial service such as America On-Line or CompuServe is another, more expensive source of information. See *Mayfield's Quick View Guide to the Internet for Students of Intimate Relationships, Sexuality, and Marriage and the Family* for more information.

The Structure of Scholarly Articles

Scholarly articles generally have six sections: Abstract, Introduction, Methods, Results, Discussion, and References. These sections may be briefly described as follows:

Abstract—summarizes the article. It briefly give you the hypothesis, theories, methodology, results, and interpretation of the findings.

Introduction—discusses the topic, reviews previous research, and states the study's hypothesis and predictions.

Methods—describes how the research was conducted. It is usually broken up into three subsections: (1) Subjects, describing the people studied; (2) Materials, describing materials used in the study; and (3) Procedure, describing how the study was done.

Results—gives the results of the research. It provides the statistics and quantitative results.

Discussion—refers to ideas, hypotheses, and studies examined in the Introduction; it also suggests future research or argues for or against a theory.

References—provides a bibliography of the article's sources.

Useful Reading Tips

1. *Read the Abstract first.* The Abstract gives you a general idea of what to expect.

2. *Scan the article.* This will give you a feel for what is being covered.

3. *Skip around.* You don't have to read the article in any particular order. Reading the Introduction and Discussion sections first often makes it easier to understand the article.

4. *Read the article at least twice.* Don't think that something is wrong with you if you don't understand everything after the first reading. Scholarly articles are difficult.

5. *Read the Methods and Results sections for general information.* Usually all you need to know from these sections is how the research was conducted and what its results were. You usually don't need to know every detail.

6. *Think critically.* Just because an article is scholarly doesn't mean it is without errors or biases. Its research, for example, may not support its conclusions.

Evaluating the Article

In evaluating a journal article, keep in mind the following considerations about research samples and methodological limitations. Chapter 2 goes into greater detail about these issues.

Sampling Issues. The choice of a sample is critical. To be useful, a sample should be representative, meaning that this small group represents a larger group in terms of age, sex, ethnicity, social class, orientation, and so on. Samples that are not representative of the larger group are known as biased samples. Most samples in sex research are limited because they depend on volunteers; their subjects are usually young, middle-class college students; and ethnic groups are generally underrepresented.

Clinical Research. A major limitation of clinical research is its focus on unhealthy behavior. Ask yourself (1) the basis on which a condition was defined as healthy or unhealthy, (2) whether inferences gathered from the behavior of patients can be applied to others, and (3) whether the individuals are representative of the group.

Survey Research. Limitations of survey research include (1) people inaccurately reporting their sexual behavior; (2) interviewers allowing preconceptions to influence the way they frame their questions, thereby biasing their interpretations; (3) the discomfort some respondents feel about revealing sexual information; (4) the interviewer's gender, which may influence respondents' comfort level; and (5) the reluctance of some ethnic groups to reveal sexual information.

Observational Research. Limitations of observational research include (1) volunteer bias, (2) whether awareness of being observed affects behaviors, (3) whether participant observation affects objectivity, and (4) ethical responsibilities regarding informing those being studied.

Experimental Research. Concerns about experimental research include (1) whether the experiment adequately replicates real-life situations, (2) how devices used to measure sexual response affect responsiveness, (3) whether genital response accurately reflects sexual/erotic response, and (4) whether experimental results can be generalized to nonlaboratory conditions.

Differences in sampling and methodological techniques help explain why scientific studies of the same phenomenon may arrive at different conclusions. Sometimes conclusions differ because of errors concerning different assumptions about human sexuality.

Journals

If we were to choose only five journals with which to keep up with the field, they would be the ones listed below in alphabetical order. They should be part of your library's basic journal collection. (If not, see if they will acquire the missing titles.)

Archives of Sexual Behavior

Family Planning Perspectives

Journal of Homosexuality

Journal of Sex and Marital Therapy

Journal of Sex Research

Other useful journals are listed below. A few are specifically related to human sexuality, but because they are not usually found in college or university library collections, we have listed them here. Most of the journals are not directly related to human sexuality but often have relevant articles.

Adolescence

American Journal of Public Health

Family Life Educator

Family Relations

Health Educator

Hispanic Journal of Behavioral Sciences

JAMA: Journal of the American Medical Association

Journal of American Public Health

Journal of Black Psychology

Journal of Black Studies

Journal of Marital and Family Therapy

Journal of Marriage and the Family

Journal of Psychology and Human Sexuality

Journal of Sex Education and Therapy

Journal of Social Issues

Journal of Social and Personal Relationships

Journal of Social Work and Human Sexuality

Journal of the History of Sexuality

New England Journal of Medicine

Sage: A Scholarly Journal of Black Women

Sex Roles

Sexually Transmitted Diseases

SIECUS Reports

Women and Health

WRITING A RESEARCH PAPER

There are nine basic steps to writing a research paper. The following will help guide you through the decisions you will need to make and tasks you will need to accomplish in writing a research paper. Notice that actually writing the paper doesn't occur until step eight.

Step One: Start with an idea that interests you. Begin with a subject, idea, or question that you find interesting. Because you may be spending considerable time working on it, make sure it's not boring. This initial idea may evolve into something entirely different, but you need to find a starting point.

Step Two: Make sure your idea is doable. Once you've found an idea that interests you, do some background reading and researching to get a feel for the topic. See what research has been done. Talk with your instructor or teaching assistant to make sure that your topic is doable, that is, that it's not too general, there are available resources, and so on.

Step Three: Create a bibliography. After you know your idea is doable, create a bibliography on your topic. Use general bibliographies of scholarly articles, such as *Sociological Abstracts* or *Psychological Abstracts,* or do a search on computer bibliographic databases, such as PsycLit and Sociofile. Your reference librarian will be glad to assist you.

Step Four: Read relevant articles and books. Read other works on your topic to find whether (1) your idea has already been researched, (2) other research changes what you want to do, and (3) you can incorporate earlier research into your paper.

Step Five: Decide on your methodology. Decide which methodology you will use: survey, observational, clinical, or experimental. In Chapter 2 of the text you'll find a discussion of the different methods that may help you decide on your methodology.

Step Six: Write an outline. Writing an outline will help you organize your ideas and clarify the steps you will need to do in your research. Remember, however, that writing a research paper is an evolving process. You will probably change your outline as you go along.

Step Seven: Conduct your research. At this point you need to conduct your actual research. This involves constructing the materials for the survey or experiment; planning how to conduct the survey, interviews, observation, or experiment; and collecting the data.

Step Eight: Write your paper. Use your outline to write a first draft. If you use the American Psychological Association style, your paper will be divided into six parts (see "The Structure of Scholarly Articles").

Step Nine: Rewrite. Rewriting is the key to good writing. After you've written your paper, put it aside for a few days, then come back to it fresh and reread it, pencil in hand. (If you've input the paper on a computer, read the hard copy.)

An excellent technique for refining your paper is to read it aloud. Reading it aloud will help you "hear" awkward sentences, bad grammar, incomplete sentences; it will help you "see" typos and misspellings.

Show your paper to a friend and ask for his or her reactions: Is the paper well organized? Is it complete? Does it read smoothly?

Finally, retype your paper. Be sure that you have corrected all typographical and spelling errors. A carefully typed or printed paper reflects the care you put into your project.

RESEARCHING AND NETWORKING WITH COMPUTERS

Using computers is a great way to gather information and expand your knowledge. In the last decade, using the Internet via computers and online services has provided a new way to gather information and a new forum for the discussion of special interest topics with others. While it may take some time and energy to get started, the rewards are certainly worth the effort. This brief overview of what is available can get you started.

Electronic Mail Many schools have access to electronic mail and will establish your own account with an address. E-mail addresses usually look like this: *jsmith@csulb.edu*. The first part (*jsmith*) is the user's identification. The next two parts make up the address "domain," or location of the computer that the user's mail will be delivered through. In this case *csulb* stands for California State University, Long Beach. It could be a company name like *apple* (Apple Computers) or a service like *aol* (America On-Line.) The second part of the domain indicates the computer server as *edu* for an educational institution, *com* for a commercial organization, *gov* for a government site, or *net* for a network provider. If you get an account at your school or through a private service like AOL, you can write to anyone else who has e-mail anywhere in the world. It's a wonderful way to stay in touch with friends and family, as well as to network with people professionally.

The World Wide Web The World Wide Web has quickly become the most popular part of the Internet. Many sites have graphics, sound, and even video. Your school or Internet service will have Web browser programs to help you cruise the Web. To get to an information source, you need to know the site's address. This is known as a URL (Uniform Resource Locator). For example, the URL for the National Institutes of Health looks like this: *http://www.nih.gov/*. There are also "search engines" that allow you to search for a specific topic. These engines will give you a list of sites with more information on your topic, and will allow you to "link" to the sites automatically. Many Web sites have "links" you click on to get to additional related Web pages. Some of these search engines include Yahoo, Webcrawler, and AltaVista. You can ask at your school computer lab how to get these or other services that will help you find information on a specific topic.

Here are some Web sites you can visit to find information related to human sexuality.

http://www.agi-usa.org The Alan Guttmacher Institute runs this site providing information on birth control and other aspects of reproductive health. It also has links to other sites with related information.

http://www.apa.org The American Psychological Association has an excellent site that includes a searchable database of abstracts on over 1,350 scholarly journals.

http://www.psych-web.com/ This site contains a database of psychology-related resources, Web links, and self-help resources.

http://www.siecus.org/ This site, run by the Sexuality Information and Education Council of the United States (SIECUS), has information on many topics related to sexuality.

http://www.goodvibes.com/ This is the site of a store that sells sex toys. However, it contains some useful information about sexual health.

Computer Listservs These are various types of lists, created for scholars, researchers, activists, and general discussion groups. Subscribe to these and the discussion will be delivered to your e-mail address automatically. Examples of computer lists related to human sexuality include:

INFO-AIDS is an AIDS information mailing list. To subscribe, send requests to info-Aids@rainbow.uucp.edu

MAIL-MEN is a discussion list on men's issues for men and women. To subscribe, send requests to MAIL-MEN-REQUEST@ATTUNIX.ATT.COM

WMN-HLTH is a Woman's Health Electronic News Line maintained by the Center for Women's Health Research. Send subscription requests to LISTSERV@UWAVM.U.WASHINGTON.EDU

If you have problems sending mail to these lists, ask someone at the computer lab in your school for help.

USENET Newsgroups USENET is a conferencing discussion network. The discussions are organized into newsgroups, and there are thousands of such groups discussing topics from rock music or television shows to cooking or health issues to just about anything else you could imagine. There are many newsgroups that have discussions related to human sexuality, gender, health issues, and other health-related topics. Many groups whose names begin with "alt.sex" deal with sexual issues. The methods of accessing USENET newgroups vary, so ask the computer people at your school how to access them on your system. (Services like AOL and Prodigy also have newsgroups on different areas of interest.) Some examples of newsgroups related to sexuality are:

alt.politics.homosexuality—Political discussions of homosexuality

alt.politics.sex—Political discussions related to sexual issues

alt.sexual.abuse.recovery—Discussion, self-help group related to issues for those who have experienced sexual abuse

Many of these groups are not regulated or moderated in any way, which may help you to understand the concerns that individuals and government officials have about this means of communication. Groups come and go, so you may find the groups above no longer exist.

This is just a small part of what the Internet makes available as a way of enhancing your research techniques. As you examine these sources of information, you must remember the importance of evaluating the information you find, as discussed in Chapter 2 of the textbook.

This is even more important when using information from the Internet. Since there is no regulating body that monitors the reliability of what is on the Internet, it is not always easy to tell what is reliable information and what is not. Here are some guidelines to help you evaluate what you find.

Who is the author or sponsor of the page?
> The individual or organization that sponsors a page should be identified, as well as their qualifications given. There should be some way to verify their reputation, such as an address or way to contact them. It is a good idea to start with a reputable source such as a research institute or established professional organization.

What is the purpose of the page?
> Is this site set up as a public service, a research tool for academics or students, or does the person have a personal ax to grind? Some sites that look informational may be trying to sell a product.

How well maintained is the page?
> Some sites are set up and then not maintained or changed to include new information. Many pages add a "last updated" note on the page, so you can see how recent the information is.

Is the information primary or secondary, and can it be verified?
> Primary information, such as a journal article, is usually preferred to secondary information, such as a review interpreting the material from the original article. Does the site have a bibliography where you can check the information against a source in the library?

AMERICAN PSYCHOLOGICAL ASSOCIATION STYLE:
A QUICK REFERENCE

Preparing the Reference List or Bibliograph

Indent the first line of each reference five spaces. Each subsequent line is flush left. Specific pages or sections of non-edited books (where the whole book is written by the author(s)) are referred to within the text of the paper, not in the reference list.

Book:
     Lastname, A. B. (year). <u>Book title underlined: Only first word and first word after a colon are capitalized.</u> City, AB: Publisher's Name.
(Capitalize proper names. Use Postal Service two-letter abbreviation for states. Use only initials for first and middle names.)

Book other than the first edition:
     Lastname, A. B. (19xx). <u>Book title</u> (3rd ed.). Publishing City, YZ: Publisher.

Article in a journal:
     Lastname, A. B., & Another, A. B. (19xx). Article title is not underlined: First words only are capitalized. <u>Journal Title Underlined with Main Words Capitalized, 12,</u> 15–35.
(Note that the volume number is underlined with page numbers following. A journal is a periodical for professional and scholarly papers. It is not a magazine.)

Article in a journal with issues paginated separately:
     Lastname, A. B., Another, A. B., & More, Y. Z. (19xx). Article title. <u>Journal Title, 12</u>(3), 15–35.
(Note that the issue number is included only if each issue begins with page 1. Note how multiple authors are listed.)

Article in an edited book:
     Lastname, A. B. (19xx). Article name as for a journal article. In Y. Z. Somebody (Ed.), <u>Name of book written as for a book above</u> (pp. 200–300). City, XY: Publisher.
(Note that the page numbers for the article are within parentheses and preceded by "pp." An edited book may contain works by many different authors.)

Article in a magazine:
     Lastname, A. B. (19xx, Month). Article name as for a journal article. <u>Magazine Name as for a Journal,</u> pp. 12–14, 76–77.
(Note that no volume or issue number is used. If an article appears on discontinuous pages, note all pages. If the magazine is published more frequently than once a month, include the date after the month.)

Article in a newspaper:
     Lastname, A. B. (19xx, Month date). Article title. <u>Name of Newspaper,</u> pp. 1, 12–13.

Article with no author given:
     Article title written as usual. (19xx, Month date). <u>Name of Newspaper,</u> p. 10.

Nonprint Media such as Film, Videotapes, and Audiotapes:
     Lastname, A. B. (Producer) & Lastname, A. C. (Director). (1979) <u>Title of the film</u> [Film] City of distributor, State: Distributor.
Give the name and, in parentheses, the function of the originator or primary contributors. Specify the medium in brackets immediately following the title. Other nonprint media such as videotapes, audiotapes, slides, charts, or artwork work can also be listed this way.

CD-ROMs:

 Lastname, A. B. <u>Title of CD Is Underlined</u> [CD-ROM]. (19xx). Production City, AZ [Producer and distributor]

Television Broadcast:

 Lastname, A. (Executive Producer). (1996, June 11). Name of television show. Place it originated: Network.

Online Sources:

At the present time APA style for referencing online information is still evolving. However, as with other references, the goal is to give credit to the author and to make it possible for the reader to find the material.

Use the author's name if available, title of the source, and date. Include identification of the type of document, such as [Personal home page]. In place of a publisher is the complete URL underlined. If the URL will not fit on one line, break it after a period or slash. Finally, the entry should include in parentheses the date you visited the page. While all of this information may not be available, include as much as possible so your source can be found.

SEICUS (1998, October 31) Helping parents be better sex educators. URL http://www.seicus.org/ (visited 1998, December 10)

Consult http://www.apa.org/journals/webref.html for up-to-date guidelines from the American Psychological Association on citing materials from the Internet.

Citing Sources Within the Text

Follow any idea or findings you report from another source after stating it (Lastname, 19xx).

If you state the findings using the author's name within the text, put only the year in parentheses after the statement which includes the author's last name (19xx).

One study concluded, "Direct quotes must include page number" (Lastname, 19xx, p. 20).

When only a section or chapter of an unedited book is being referenced, put inclusive pages in the text, not in the reference list (Author, 19xx, pp. 200–300).

Use only the author's last name, unless there are two authors in the reference list with the same last name (A. B. Smith, 19xx) and (X. Y. Smith, 19xx).

When referencing more than one study after a single idea, separate each reference by a semicolon (Smith & Roger, 19xx; Jones, 19xx).

When referencing an article with no author, use a shortened form of the title within quotes ("Study Finds," 19xx).

When referencing an article with more than two authors, cite all authors the first time; for subsequent citations, use the first author followed by "et al." (Adams, Smith, and Brown, 19xx) becomes (Adams et al., 19xx).

Consult the <u>Publication Manual of the American Psychological Association,</u> which is in most libraries, if you have any questions.

PART IV

ANSWERS TO PRACTICE TEST QUESTIONS

ANSWERS TO PRACTICE TEST QUESTIONS

Chapter 1 — Perspectives on Human Sexuality

Multiple Choice	True/False	Fill-In	Short Answers
1. d	1. F	1. entertainment	1. See pages 9–22
2. c	2. T	2. norms	2. See pages 22–27
3. c	3. F	3. two-spirit	3. See pages 27–32
4. b	4. F	4. sexual impulses	
5. d	5. T	5. heterosexuality	
6. c	6. F	6. sexual orientation	
7. c	7. T	7. transsexuals	
8. a	8. T	8. normal	
9. a	9. T	9. sexual variation	
10. d	10. F	10. continuum	
11. a			
12. a			

Chapter 2 — Studying Human Sexuality

Multiple Choice	Fill-In	Matching	Short Answers
1. d	1. sex information/advice genre	1. c	1. See pages 39–43
2. a	2. value judgments	2. b	2. See page 44
3. b	3. acculturation	3. e	3. See pages 62–68
4. a	4. objectivity	4. f	
5. c	5. ethnocentric	5. d	
6. a	6. informed consent	6. g	
7. b	7. biased	7. a	
8. d	8. pathological		
9. b	9. survey		
10. d	10. phallic		
11. a	11. autoeroticism		
12. d			
13. b			
14. a			
15. c			

Chapter 3 Female Sexual Anatomy, Physiology, and Response

Multiple Choice	Fill-In	Short Answers
1. b	1. clitoris	1. See pages 88, 90
2. a	2. Bartholin's glands	2. See page 93
3. d	3. introitus	3. See pages 94
4. a	4. endometrium	
5. a	5. ovulation	
6. b	6. hormones	
7. a	7. XX	
8. a	8. dysmenorrhea	
9. b	9. amenorrhea	
10. d	10. erogenous zones	
11. a	11. pheromones	
12. c	12. libido	
13. b	13. vasocongestion and myotonia	
14. a	14. sweating	
15. c	15. orgasm	

Female Sexual Anatomy Diagrams

A. Internal	B. External	C. Female Breast
1. (e) fallopian tube	1. (d) labia majora	1. (g) nipple
2. (h) ovary	2. (h) opening of the urethra	2. (b) areola
3. (m) uterus	3. (f) mons pubis	3. (i) suspensory ligaments
4. (b) bladder	4. (b) clitoral hood	4. (d) fat
5. (i) pubic bone	5. (c) clitoris (glans)	5. (b) areola
6. (k) urethra	6. (e) labia minora	6. (g) nipple
7. (d) clitoris	7. (i) vaginal opening	7. (f) milk ducts
8. (l) urinary opening	8. (g) perineum	8. (h) ribs
9. (f) labia majora	9. (a) anus	9. (c) chest wall
10. (c) cervix		10. (e) lobes
11. (j) rectum		11. (a) alveoli
12. (n) vagina		
13. (a) anus		
14. (o) vaginal opening		
15. (g) labia minora		

Chapter 4   Male Sexual Anatomy, Physiology, and Response

Multiple Choice	Fill-In	Short Answers
1. d	1. frenulum	1. See page 105
2. b	2. circumcision	2. See pages 106–108
3. a	3. smegma	3. See pages 109
4. b	4. testicles	
5. c	5. testosterone	
6. a	6. spermatogenesis	
7. a	7. brain-testicular axis	
8. c	8. semen	
9. a	9. ejaculatory inevitability	
10. b	10. refractory period	
11. a		
12. d		

Male Sexual Anatomy Diagrams

A. Internal

1. (b) bladder
2. (i) pubic bone
3. (o) vas deferens
4. (c) corpus spongiosum
5. (g) penis
6. (n) urethra
7. (f) opening of the urethra
8. (l) seminal vesicle
9. (j) rectum
10. (h) prostate
11. (d) Cowper's gland
12. (a) anus
13. (e) epididymis
14. (m) testis
15. (j) scrotum

B. External

1. (a) circumcised
2. (b) uncircumcised
3. (e) shaft of penis
4. (f) testes (in scrotum)
5. (d) glands
6. (g) opening of the urethra
7. (c) foreskin

C. Cross Section

1. (a) corposa cavernosa
2. (b) corpus spongiosum
3. (g) urethra
4. (d) head of epididymis
5. (h) vas deferens
6. (c) epididymis
7. (e) seminiferous tubules
8. (f) tail of epididymis

Chapter 5   Gender and Gender Roles

Multiple Choice	Fill-In	Matching	Short Answers
1. c	1. gender identity	1. b	1. See page 122
2. a	2. anatomical sex	2. d	2. See pages 130–132
3. b	3. script	3. a	3. See page 134
4. d	4. sociobiology	4. f	
5. c	5. reinforcement/modeling	5. c	
6. d	6. schema	6. e	
7. b	7. female		
8. d	8. androgyny		
9. b	9. gender dysphoria		
10. d	10. transsexuals		
11. c			
12. b			
13. a			
14. b			
15. b			

Chapter 6   Sexuality Over The Life Span

Multiple Choice	True/False	Fill-In	Short Answers
1. a	1. T	1. inappropriate	1. See page 151
2. c	2. F	2. menstruation/ejaculation	2. See pages 162–163
3. a	3. T	3. puberty	3. See page 165
4. d	4. T	4. adolescence	4. See pages 173
5. b	5. T	5. psychosexual	5. See pages 184–185
6. c	6. F	6. homosociality	
7. d	7. F	7. heterosociality	
8. b	8. T	8. nonmarital	
9. a	9. T	9. premarital	
10. b	10. F	10. swinging	
11. c		11. open marriage	
12. b			
13. a			
14. c			

Chapter 7   Love, Intimacy, and Sexuality

Multiple Choice

1. d
2. a
3. d
4. d
5. c
6. d
7. d
8. c
9. d
10. a
11. a
12. b
13. a
14. b
15. c

Fill-In

1. prototypes
2. suspicious
3. commitment
4. infatuation
5. romantic love
6. attachment
7. reactive
8. self-disclosure
9. caring
10. jealousy

Matching

1. c
2. f
3. e
4. a
5. b
6. d

Short Answers

1. See pages 203–305
2. See pages 209–213
3. See pages 219–221

Chapter 8   Communicating About Sex

Multiple Choice

1. d
2. d
3. a
4. c
5. d
6. b
7. c
8. d
9. a
10. d
11. c

True/False

1. T
2. T
3. F
4. T
5. F
6. T
7. T
8. F
9. F
10. T
11. F

Fill-In

1. communication
2. self-disclosure
3. agreement
4. proximity
5. halo effect
6. vocabulary
7. feedback
8. trust
9. status
10. principle of least interest
11. power
12. relative love and need

Short Answers

1. See pages 238–240
2. See pages 240–241
3. See pages 250–251

Chapter 9   Sexual Expression

Multiple Choice

1. b
2. c
3. c
4. a
5. a
6. a
7. d
8. c
9. d
10. d

True/False

1. F
2. T
3. T
4. T
5. F
6. T
7. F
8. T
9. F
10. F

Fill-In

1. sexual scripts
2. autoeroticism
3. erotophilia
4. woman above
5. pleasuring
6. kissing
7. cunnilingus
8. fellatio
9. analingus
10. masturbation

Short Answers

1. See pages 260–262
2. See pages 263–264
3. See pages 265–271
4. See page 271

Chapter 10   Atypical and Paraphilic Sexual Behavior

Multiple Choice

1. c
2. a
3. b
4. d
5. a
6. b
7. d
8. c
9. b
10. c
11. c
12. b

True/False

1. F
2. F
3. F
4. F
5. T
6. T
7. F
8. F
9. F
10. F

Fill-In

1. nymphomania
2. domination and submission
3. dominatrix
4. fetishism
5. zoophilia
6. frotteurism
7. voyeurism
8. exhibitionism
9. pedophilia
10. autoerotic asphyxia

Short Answers

1. See pages 293–298
2. See page 301
3. See pages 303–304

Chapter 11   Contraception and Birth Control

Multiple Choice

1. d
2. c
3. c
4. c
5. d
6. c
7. a
8. d
9. c
10. b
11. c
12. b
13. c
14. b
15. d

Fill-In

1. birth control/contraception
2. abstinence
3. latex or polyurethane condom
4. fertility awareness
5. diaphragm/cervical cap
6. laminaria
7. vacuum aspiration
8. sterilization
9. dilation and evacuation
10. hysterectomy

Matching

1. e
2. c
3. f
4. a
5. b
6. h
7. d
8. g

Short Answers

1. See page 311
2. See pages 317–321
3. See page 326
4. See pages 348–349

Chapter 12 Conception, Pregnancy, and Childbirth

Multiple Choice	Fill-In	Matching 1	Short Answers
1. b	1. teratogens	1. b	1. See pages 360–363
2. d	2. ectopic	2. a	2. See page 362
3. b	3. in vitro fertilization	3. c	3. See pages 369–371
4. d	4. gamete intrafallopian transfer	4. g	4. See pages 373–378
5. c	5. artificial insemination	5. e	
6. a	6. amniocentesis	6. f	
7. c	7. surrogate motherhood	7. d	
8. c	8. effacement		**The Fetus**
9. d	9. dilation	**Matching 2**	**and Placenta**
10. c	10. episiotomy	1. c	1. f
11. a		2. e	2. k
12. d		3. b	3. b
13. c		4. a	4. j
14. a		5. d	5. c
15. a			6. q
		Matching 3	7. a
		1. c	8. d
		2. d	9. p
		3. e	10. n
		4. b	11. l
		5. a	12. e
			13. g
			14. h
			15. i
			16. o
			17. m

Chapter 13 The Sexual Body In Health and Illness

Multiple Choice	True/False	Fill-In	Short Answers
1. a	1. T	1. bulimia/anorexia nervosa	1. See pages 404–407
2. c	2. F	2. endometriosis	2. See pages 410–412
3. b	3. T	3. menopause	3. See pages 412–413
4. c	4. F	4. osteoporosis	4. See pages 414–420
5. a	5. T	5. hormone replacement	and 420–422
6. c	6. F	6. benign/malignant	
7. c	7. F	7. breast self-examination/mammograms	
8. d	8. T	8. mastectomy/lumpectomy	
9. b	9. F	9. Pap test	
10. c	10. T	10. hysterectomy	
11. c		11. toxic shock syndrome	
12. a		12. prostatitis	
13. b		13. disinhibition	
14. a			
15. d			

Chapter 14   Sexual Enhancement and Therapy

Multiple Choice	True/False	Fill-In	Short Answers
1. c	1. F	1. sexual aversion	1. See pages 432–433
2. b	2. F	2. dyspareunia	2. See page 448
3. c	3. T	3. anorgasmia	3. See pages 451–454
4. b	4. T	4. squeeze technique	
5. a	5. F	5. premature ejaculation	
6. d	6. T	6. spectatoring	
7. c	7. T	7. sensate focus	
8. a	8. T	8. vaginismus	
9. d	9. F	9. PLISSIT	
10. c	10. T		
11. a			
12. a			
13. c			
14. a			

Chapter 15   Sexually Transmitted Diseases

Multiple Choice	True/False	Fill-In	Short Answers
1. d	1. T	1. candidiasis	1. See pages 464–465
2. b	2. F	2. chancre	2. See page 466
3. b	3. F	3. cystitis	3. See page 481
4. c	4. T	4. chlamydia	4. See pages 483–486
5. c	5. T	5. gonorrhea	
6. b	6. F	6. genital warts	
7. a	7. T	7. prodrome	
8. c	8. F	8. syphilis	
9. c	9. F	9. hepatitis	
10. b	10. T	10. asymptomatic	

Chapter 16   HIV and AIDS

Multiple Choice	True/False	Fill-In	Short Answers
1. b	1. F	1. acquired immune deficiency syndrome	1. See pages 490–492
2. a	2. F	2. opportunistic infections	2. See pages 499–500
3. a	3. F	3. Kaposi's sarcoma	3. See page 503
4. c	4. T	4. antigens	
5. c	5. F	5. retroviruses	
6. a	6. T	6. seroconversion	
7. c	7. F	7. wasting syndrome	
8. b	8. T	8. parenteral transmission	
9. a	9. T	9. perinatal transmission	
10. d	10. T	10. ELISA	
11. c			
12. d			

Chapter 17   Sexual Coercion: Harassment, Aggression, and Abuse

Multiple Choice	True/False	Fill-In	Short Answers
1. d	1. F	1. sexual harassment	1. See pages 524–528
2. c	2. T	2. heterosexual bias	2. See pages 528–529
3. d	3. F	3. Sexual aggression	3. See pages 542–544
4. b	4. F	4. date rape, acquaintance rape	4. See pages 547–551
5. a	5. T	5. statutory rape	
6. b	6. T	6. rape trauma syndrome	
7. b	7. F	7. child sexual abuse	
8. c	8. T	8. intrafamilial abuse	
9. a	9. F	9. gay bashing	
10. b	10. T	10. incest	
11. d			

Chapter 18   Commercial Sex

Multiple Choice	True/False	Fill-In	Short Answers
1. d	1. T	1. erotica	1. See page 566
2. c	2. F	2. pornography	2. See pages 559–560
3. c	3. T	3. sexually oriented	3. See page 563
4. d	4. T	4. sexually explicit	
5. d	5. F	5. cyberporn	
6. b	6. T	6. femme porn	
7. a	7. T	7. censorship	
8. c	8. F	8. obscenity	
9. d	9. F	9. subculture	
10. c	10. T	10. peer delinquent	

VALUES SURVEY REVIEW

Long, long ago (at the beginning of the semester!) you were asked to complete a values survey (Looking at Your Values in Chapter 2 of this book). Without looking back at your responses, again answer these questions.

SA   CIRCLE IF YOU STRONGLY AGREE

A   CIRCLE IF YOU MODERATELY AGREE

U   CIRCLE IF YOU ARE UNDECIDED, OR HAVE NO OPINION

D   CIRCLE IF YOU MODERATELY DISAGREE

SD   CIRCLE IF YOU STRONGLY DISAGREE

FEMALE _____

MALE _____

STATEMENT
LEVEL OF AGREEMENT

	STATEMENT	SA	A	U	D	SD
A.	You should have sex only with someone you love.	SA	A	U	D	SD
B.	Masturbation is a healthy, acceptable form of sexual behavior.	SA	A	U	D	SD
C.	A woman should feel able to be as sexually assertive as a man.	SA	A	U	D	SD
D.	Abortions should be available to any woman who desires to terminate a pregnancy.	SA	A	U	D	SD
E.	Transvestites are psychologically dysfunctional.	SA	A	U	D	SD
F.	Prostitution should be a crime.	SA	A	U	D	SD
G.	Magazines like *Penthouse* and *Playboy* should be available at liquor stores.	SA	A	U	D	SD
H.	Homosexuality is unnatural and immoral.	SA	A	U	D	SD
I.	High school clinics should provide birth control.	SA	A	U	D	SD
J.	All doctors should be tested for HIV, and patients notified of status.	SA	A	U	D	SD
K.	Parents should be notified and give permission before their daughters can have an abortion.	SA	A	U	D	SD
L.	All hospital patients should be tested for HIV, and doctors notified of status.	SA	A	U	D	SD
M.	If a 15-year-old boy has consensual sex with a 20-year-old female, she should be arrested.	SA	A	U	D	SD
N.	If a 15-year-old girl has consensual sex with a 20-year-old male, he should be arrested.	SA	A	U	D	SD
O.	Surrogate motherhood should be legal.	SA	A	U	D	SD
P.	Rape is often charged because women regret what they did.	SA	A	U	D	SD
Q.	A boy who has not had sex by the time he is 17 is weird.	SA	A	U	D	SD

Compare the results from the beginning of the semester to now. How are they similar or different?

What do you feel influenced any changes?

How might your survey have appeared if you had taken it two years ago?

In what direction do you feel your values are moving?

How do you think your parents might answer these questions?

What about your best friend or partner?

If you would like, ask a trusted person to complete the survey and discuss the responses with him or her.

A FINAL MESSAGE TO STUDENTS

Tell Us What You Think

The authors of this Study Guide hope that it has been beneficial for you. The best way we can improve it is by your feedback. We would like to hear from you. You can fill out this form and mail it to us or you can contact us through the Internet at bobbim@csulb.edu.

Male _____   Female _____   Age _____   Date _____

School _____

Instructor _____

1. What parts of the Study Guide did you use?

	ALWAYS	USUALLY	SOMETIMES	1–2 TIMES	NEVER
Learning Objectives					
Multiple Choice					
True-False/Matching					
Key Term Fill-Ins					
Short Answer Questions					
Reflections					
Observations					
Gender and Sexual Identity Questions					

2. What parts of the Study Guide were most helpful?

3. What parts of the Study Guide were least helpful?

4. What other assignments or materials would you like to see included in this Study Guide?

5. Did your instructor have you do any of the observations or reflections for the class? If yes, which one(s)?

6. Did you share the personal exercises in the book with others (partner, parents, friends, etc.)?

7. If yes to Question 6, what was their reaction, and what was the result?

8. Did you do the sexual identity assignment for your own information or for a class assignment?

9. What other comments do you have about the book?